Deborah

THE EPIC OF EDEN

Deborah

UNLIKELY HEROES AND THE BOOK OF JUDGES

EIGHT-SESSION BIBLE STUDY GUIDE

SANDRA L. RICHTER

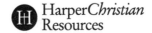
Harper*Christian*
Resources

Epic of Eden: Deborah Bible Study Guide
Copyright © 2024 by Sandra L. Richter

Published in Grand Rapids, Michigan, by HarperChristian Resources. HarperChristian Resources is a registered trademark of HarperCollins Christian Publishing, Inc.

Requests for information should be addressed to customercare@harpercollins.com.

ISBN 978-0-310-16649-8 (softcover)
ISBN 978-0-310-16650-4 (ebook)

HarperChristian Resources titles may be purchased in bulk for church, business, fundraising, or ministry use. For information, please email ResourceSpecialist@ChurchSource.com.

First Printing June 2024 / Printed in the United States of America

24 25 26 27 28 29 30 31 32 33 34 /TRM/ 16 15 14 13 12 11 10 9 8 7 6 5 4 3 2 1

Contents

Acknowledgments

As always, this *Epic of Eden* study of Deborah and the book of Judges is dedicated to all the students with whom I have had the privilege of learning this material. I am especially grateful for the communities who allowed me to test-drive this curriculum with them while it was unfolding! For the good folk of Redwood Christian Park in Boulder Creek, CA; Trinity Methodist Church in Ruston, LA; Douglasville United Methodist Church in Douglasville, GA; Faith Methodist Church in Richmond, TX; and Santa Barbara Community Church in Santa Barbara, CA: not only did I so enjoy my time with you, but I am forever grateful for your input. Deborah's story is indeed a "story that matters," and studying this epic tale of courage and commitment has been a gift to me. My dearest hope is that this deep dive into the stouthearted faith of Deborah, Barak, Naphtali, and Zebulun will bring each of us the courage we need as we battle for the kingdom on our side of the cross.

This project could not have been completed without the colossal investment of many people. My deepest gratitude to Sara Riemersma, senior acquisitions editor and general mastermind of Zondervan/HarperChristian Resources, for her enthusiastic vision and masterful coordination of this project. Sara's tireless editing of video, text, and content is matched only by her commitment to excellence. My thanks as well to John Raymond, vice president and publisher for HarperChristian Resources, for his behind-the-scenes leadership. To TJ Rathbun, Joel Riddering, and Studio Jefferson for hours (and hours) of filming, unending encouragement, super creative ideas, and being all around great guys to work with. To Becky Gohl (Rebecca.Gohl@me.com) for going above and beyond hair and makeup to accessorizing my wardrobe. And to 52 Watt for video editing that made all things beautiful. To Jeanine Strock, our visual editor, who tracked down countless images and kindly dealt with all my perfectionism to ensure that our presentation was all that it must be. Our studio team were also all so grateful for the privilege of being TJ Rathbun's (executive producer, HarperCollins Christian Publishing) nearly final project before retirement. What a joy this man was to work with! To Kathy Noftsinger, my long-journey co-laborer in the Epic dream. Kathy's dedication to these projects, as they morph from vision to video, is a constant source of strength, insight, and encouragement, and I am deeply grateful.

Last but not least, to my beloved Steven, Noël, and Elise, who have paid the price of too many late nights and weekends away to bring this curriculum to its current state, my forever thanks. And to every pastor and lay leader who diligently offers the Word of God to the people of God, laboring late into the night to make sure she or he is telling the Story and telling it well, Godspeed to you. I'm with you.

Schedule to Follow

SESSION 1

GROUP MEETING
- Distribute study guides
- Watch Video Session 1—Setting the Stage in Real Time & Space
- Use streaming video access instruction on inside front cover or DVD
- Discuss video teaching

INDIVIDUAL STUDY
- Setting the Stage in Real Time & Space
- Arriving and Obeying Are Not the Same Thing

This content will cover both video sessions 1 and 2

SESSION 2

GROUP MEETING
- Watch Video Session 2—Arriving and Obeying Are Not the Same Thing
- Use streaming video access instruction on inside front cover or DVD
- Discuss homework and video teaching

INDIVIDUAL STUDY
- The Cycle of the Judges

SESSION 3

GROUP MEETING

- Watch Video Session 3—The Cycle of the Judges
- Use streaming video access instruction on inside front cover or DVD
- Discuss homework and video teaching

INDIVIDUAL STUDY

- Meet Deborah!

SESSION 4

GROUP MEETING

- Watch Video Session 4—Meet Deborah!
- Use streaming video access instruction on inside front cover or DVD
- Discuss homework and video teaching

INDIVIDUAL STUDY

- Deborah's Crisis in the Valley

SESSION 5

GROUP MEETING

- Watch Video Session 5—Deborah's Crisis in the Valley
- Use streaming video access instruction on inside front cover or DVD
- Discuss homework and video teaching

INDIVIDUAL STUDY

- Deborah Musters the Response

SESSION 6

GROUP MEETING

- Watch Video Session 6—Deborah Musters the Response
- Use streaming video access instruction on inside front cover or DVD
- Discuss homework and video teaching

INDIVIDUAL STUDY

- Deborah's Battle and Victory

SESSION 7

GROUP MEETING

- Watch Video Session 7—Deborah's Battle and Victory
- Use streaming video access instruction on inside front cover or DVD
- Discuss homework and video teaching

INDIVIDUAL STUDY

- Deborah's Legacy Still Matters Today

SESSION 8

GROUP MEETING

- Watch Video Session 8—Deborah's Legacy Still Matters Today
- Use streaming video access instruction on inside front cover or DVD
- Discuss homework and video teaching

How Is This Going to Work?

If your group has tackled an *Epic of Eden* study before, you're already pros. If not, here's the plan:

- This curriculum revolves around a set of eight filmed teaching sessions with me, Dr. Sandy Richter. Each study guide has streaming video access instructions printed on the inside cover. With this access, you can view the videos from any device. If you prefer, a DVD is available for purchase.

- The second component is this study guide, which contains lessons to be done individually at home whenever it fits your schedule. Three lessons focus on the upcoming week's video lecture; the fourth lesson focuses on another judge from the book of Judges. Do as much or as little as your schedule permits. No pressure, really.

- The study guide is designed so that the homework will (ideally) be completed before watching the videos.

- Once per week your group will gather to view the video teaching, talk about the individual work from the week, and engage in group discussion questions about both. Again, video is available either streaming, using the access instructions on the inside cover, or on DVD.

You may want to plan a little extra time for your first gathering as you meet each other, get your books, drink some coffee, have some snacks (a must for every gathering, really), and dive into the first video.

Introduction to Deborah and the Book of Judges

The book of Judges is a collection of twelve heroic narratives that provide us with a glimpse into Israel's earliest days in the land. This is the era of the settlement, just after Joshua's conquest. Joshua has detailed the boundaries of each tribe's inherited land, and now it is time to get out there and *possess* that land. So we find our heroes in that space between what Israel *was* (a tribal confederation moving through the wilderness under Moses's capable leadership) and what Israel *will be* (a unified nation under the stable leadership of a divinely chosen king). And as with most emerging nations, this in-between space is also a bit wild and wooly. The American frontier during the nineteenth century (a.k.a. the Wild West) is a good analogy. A time when the task of survival is the first thing on everyone's mind, the regular rules of civilized living get pushed to the side, and larger-than-life heroes wind up center stage. *This* is the era of the judges.

Who are the larger-than-life heroes who bring order to this chaotic period? That would be the judges. Othniel, Shamgar, and Ehud, to name a few. They're the lawmen (and women) who face down Israel's enemies abroad and enforce covenant law at home. In this lineup of gunslingers and superheroes, we will meet a range of characters who defend Israel by orthodox and not-so-orthodox means. We've got the mustered tribes fighting it out to defend their borders via military engagement. But we also have ox goads, jaw bones, secret assassinations, and the sort of chaos that only three hundred foxes with torches tied to their tails can create! But the hero of *this* curriculum, the Margaret Thatcher of the ancient world, the Antiope of Israel, the Ruth Bader Ginsburg of the Mosaic covenant, is none other than the judge and prophet Deborah. Her name means "to lead," and that is exactly what she does—for over forty years. Her story is found in Judges 4 and 5. Chapter 4 tells the story in prose, and chapter 5 tells the story in elegant, rousing, epic poetry. She is a wife, mother, liturgist, prophet, judge, and the commander in chief of Israel's volunteer army. And she is all these things in a deeply traditional society where one would never expect to see a woman lead. Our objective for these eight sessions is twofold: (1) to introduce you to Israel's "Wild West" through the heroic tales of the judges who worked to defend Yahweh's covenant and (2) to bring Deborah's story to life by a deep dive into Judges 4 and 5. Our final objective? To ask and answer what this ancient tale of courage and conflict might have to say to us right here, right now, today.

SESSION 1

Setting the Stage in Real Time & Space

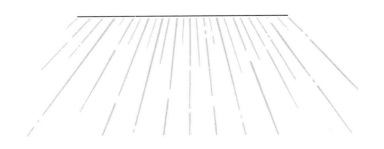

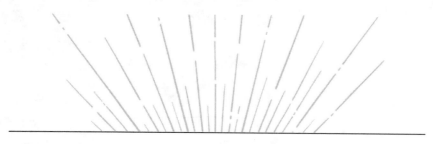

SESSION 1: GROUP MEETING

Schedule

GROUP MEETING
Session 1 Video Teaching and Discussion

INDIVIDUAL STUDY
Day 1: The Promise of Land
Day 2: Maps, Maps, Maps
Day 3: Superheroes and Scoundrels
Day 4: Meet the Judges—Othniel

Getting Started

Leader, open your group with these icebreaker questions:

- Tell the group two things you already know (or think you know) about the book of Judges coming into this study.
- Now tell the group two things you already know (or think you know) about Deborah coming into this study.
- Why did you choose this study?

Watch Session 1 Video:
Setting the Stage in Real Time & Space
[26 Minutes]

Streaming video access instructions are on the inside front cover of each study guide.

Video Outline

Follow along during the video, take notes, or write down questions and "aha" moments as you like.

   I.   Introduction to Deborah

  II. Deborah in real time

      A. Exodus

      B. Conquest

         1. Joshua 1–11: Campaigns

2. Joshua 12–24: Allotments

3. Possession

III. Deborah in real space

A. Via Maris

B. Jezreel Valley

IV. Deborah in real time

A. Our benchmarks

1. Merneptah Stela, 1208 BCE

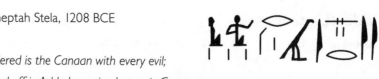

Plundered is the Canaan with every evil;
Carried off is Ashkelon; seized upon is Gezer;
Yanoam is made as that which does not exist;
Israel is laid waste, his seed is not.[1]

2. Shechem fortress temple destruction, 1100 BCE

B. Deborah somewhere between _____ BCE and _____ BCE

Merneptah Stela
© 1995 Phoenix Data Systems

---

[1] James B. Pritchard, *The Ancient Near East: Volume I, An Anthology of Texts and Pictures* (Princeton: Princeton University Press, 1958), 231.

Dialogue, Digest & Do

Discuss the following as a group.

- What aspect of Israel's **real time and space** connected with you and your world most? Why?

- Do the Israelites seem a little bit more like real people to you now? Why?

- In describing the relationship between the Old Testament and the needs of the contemporary church, I quoted Christopher J. H. Wright: "This paradigmatic nature of Israel is not just a *hermeneutical tool* devised by us retrospectively, but theologically speaking, was part of God's design in creating and shaping Israel as he did in the first place."[2] Use your phones to look up any words in here that aren't familiar, and take some time to explain this quote to each other.

- As discussed in the video, one of the great gifts of studying the narratives of redemptive history is that these ancient tales of crisis, faith, and courage offer us, the contemporary people of God, a moment when "the very real past meets the very needy present." As a group, begin the conversation as to what points of intersection you see between the story of Deborah and the "very needy present" that inhabits your world. Which challenges of God's people in the book of Judges are echoed in our contemporary challenges?

- At the end of each session, I ask the same three questions for you to consider throughout the study. So let's begin the discussion now. What territory can you see from where you're standing that belongs to the kingdom of God and, for whatever reason, is not yet in the hands of God's people? Is it worth fighting for? What are you going to do about it?

---

2 Christopher J. H. Wright, "The Ethical Authority of the Old Testament: A Survey of Approaches, Part II," *Tyndale Bulletin* 43.2 (1992): 228, https://doi.org/10.53751/001c.30489, emphasis added.

Next Week

Before next week's group meeting, do your best to tackle all four days of the individual study in your study guide. In those individual studies you'll do some important map work that will familiarize you with the **real space** of Deborah's story. You can't understand the battle that dominates the story without understanding the physical features of Deborah's homeland!

In the next group session, we'll dig into some archaeology, take a look at the structure of the book of Judges, and along the way, talk about pigs and superheroes!

Closing Prayer

Leader, ask your group members if there is anything they would like prayer for, especially something highlighted by this week's video. This would be a great time for your group to start praying for God to speak to each of you about what he wants to do with and for you through this study, and consider what making this story your own might look like.

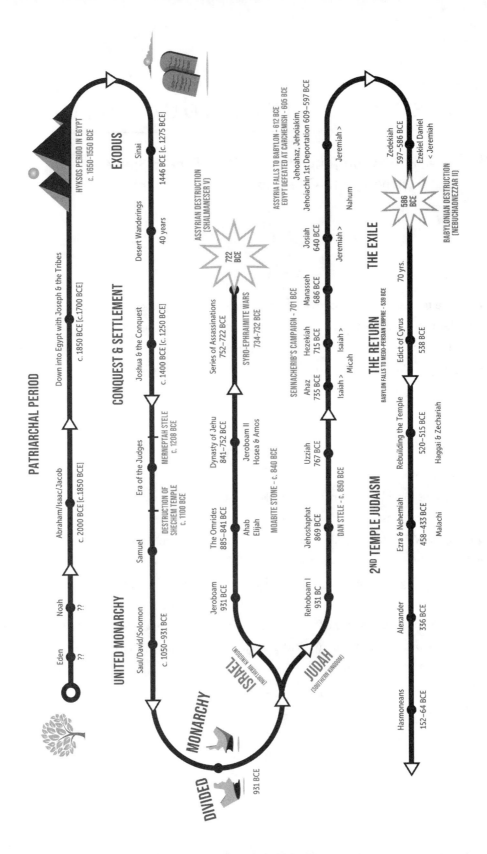

PATRIARCHAL PERIOD

Eden
??

Noah
??

Abraham/Isaac/Jacob
c. 2000 BCE [c.1850 BCE]

Down into Egypt with Joseph & the Tribes
c. 1850 BCE [c.1700 BCE]

HYKSOS PERIOD IN EGYPT
c. 1650–1550 BCE

EXODUS

Sinai

1446 BCE [c. 1275 BCE]

Desert Wanderings

40 years

CONQUEST & SETTLEMENT

Joshua & the Conquest
c. 1400 BCE [c. 1250 BCE]

MERNEPTAH STELE
c. 1208 BCE

Era of the Judges

DESTRUCTION OF
SHECHEM TEMPLE
c. 1100 BCE

Samuel

UNITED MONARCHY

Saul/David/Solomon
c. 1050–931 BCE

MONARCHY

DIVIDED
931 BCE

ISRAEL (NORTHERN KINGDOM)

Jeroboam
931 BCE

The Omrides
885–841 BCE

Ahab
Elijah

MOABITE STONE - c. 840 BCE

Dynasty of Jehu
841–752 BCE

Jeroboam II
Hosea & Amos

Series of Assassinations
752–722 BCE

SYRO-EPHRAIMITE WARS
734–732 BCE

ASSYRIAN DESTRUCTION
(SHALMANESER V)

722
BCE

JUDAH (SOUTHERN KINGDOM)

Rehoboam
931 BC

Jehoshaphat
869 BCE

DAN STELE - c. 850 BCE

Uzziah
767 BCE

Ahaz
735 BCE

< Isaiah >
Micah

Hezekiah
715 BCE

Isaiah >

SENNACHERIB'S CAMPAIGN - 701 BCE

Manasseh
686 BCE

Josiah
640 BCE

Jeremiah >

Nahum

Jeremiah >

ASSYRIA FALLS TO BABYLON - 612 BCE
EGYPT DEFEATED AT CARCHEMISH - 605 BCE

Jehoahaz, Jehoiakim,
605 BCE

Jehoiachin 1st Deportation 609–597 BCE

Zedekiah
597–586 BCE

Ezekiel Daniel
< Jeremiah

THE EXILE

586
BCE

BABYLONIAN DESTRUCTION
(NEBUCHADNEZZAR II)

70 yrs.

THE RETURN
BABYLON FALLS TO MEDO-PERSIAN EMPIRE- 539 BCE

Edict of Cyrus
538 BCE

Rebuilding the Temple
520–515 BCE

Haggai & Zechariah

Ezra & Nehemiah
458–433 BCE

Malachi

2ND TEMPLE JUDAISM

Alexander
336 BCE

Hasmoneans
152–64 BCE

SESSION 1: INDIVIDUAL STUDY

Setting the Stage in Real Time & Space
Arriving and Obeying Are Not the Same Thing

Welcome to lesson 1! The lessons found in the individual studies focus on the *upcoming* week's video lecture. Since there was no preparatory work prior to watching the session 1 video, your individual study this week will include two days of reviewing some information you heard in the video lecture. Day 3's lesson, however, will relate to the upcoming video, and day 4 (as in each of the upcoming sessions) will focus on an individual judge.

A Word from Sandy

While getting this Bible study ready for publication, I test-drove it with at least a dozen churches full of *Epic* enthusiasts. Not only did we have a blast, but I also used this time to ask over and over again, "What caught your attention? What challenged you? What made the real people and real places of this narrative come to life?" And to my joy the answer was most regularly, "The archaeology!" "The history!" "The pictures!" and even "The topography!" I had career military men rushing up during break to analyze Barak's battle strategy, the strategic advantages of Mount Tabor, and the differences between a field encounter involving infantry and one involving mobile firing platforms (we call those tanks; Barak calls them chariots). I had dozens of people who had been in the Jezreel Valley on a trip to Israel telling me tales of their encounters with that beautiful agricultural space in the wet and dry seasons, people who couldn't settle themselves until they were certain which of the peaks on their maps was Tabor and which was Gilboa. And then there were the good folk enthralled by the differences between Deborah's life in the hill country as a working mom and Jael's life as a pastoralist and stay-at-home mom. Do you know why these responses thrill me? Because they make it clear to this teacher that my students are taking the characters of the biblical narratives off the flannelgraph, out of the ivory tower, out of the land of make-believe, and putting them back into real time and space. The result is that these biblical characters become *real* people who were struggling with limited resources, pressing anxieties, and real opponents. Why does that matter? Because until these people are real to us, their stories aren't real to us either. And if their stories aren't real, neither is their faith. So I invite you, as we launch these eight weeks together, to go ahead and take Deborah and Barak, Jabin and Sisera, Heber and Jael off the flannelgraph. Take them out of the make-believe worlds we've assigned them to and put them (and their experiences with our God) back into real time and space. Learn about their families, their vocations, and their troubles. Encounter their real faith in the living God, and allow the Holy Spirit to show you where your story and their story might align. If they, with all their weaknesses and challenges, could find the faith to step forward, maybe we can too.

Day 1: The Promise of Land

Real Time & Space

In the first session's video, you heard me refer to the **Bronze Age** and the **Iron Age** in discussing the real time of Deborah and the book of Judges. These are the terms that archaeologists and historians use when they categorize the eras of Israel and Canaan's history. Each historical period has boundaries identified by major shifts in the culture of the region. And these cultural shifts were usually marked by shifts in technology, in this case the metal used for tools and weapons. Take a look at the names and dates of these historical periods and see how they connect to biblical history.

Middle Bronze Age	2000–1550 BCE	*the era of the patriarchs*
Late Bronze Age	1550–1200 BCE	*the era of the exodus and conquest*
Iron Age I	1200–1000 BCE	*the era of the settlement*
Iron Age II	1000–586 BCE	*the era of the monarchy*

When Israel first arrives in the land of Canaan under Joshua's leadership, it is the waning years of the **Late Bronze Age** (1550–1200 BCE). The **Middle Bronze Age** (when the Canaanite city states were strong and flourishing) has ended, and Egypt has been dominating the region ever since. During this **Late Bronze Age** Egyptian occupation, the political infrastructure and economy of Canaan became extremely dependent on Egypt. But at the end of the **Late Bronze Age**, Egypt begins experiencing its own domestic challenges and withdraws from Canaan. As a result, the local infrastructure and economy of Canaan, which had become dependent on the Egyptian Empire, collapses into a muddy mess. Intercity military conflict becomes normative, and landless gangs (known among the Canaanites as the *apiru*) are everywhere, looting and creating conflict. The good news? The chaos creates a window of opportunity for the Israelites to immigrate successfully. And as long as our heroes stay away from the most entrenched (and formidable) remnants of Canaanite power on the coast and in the Jezreel Valley, things go fairly smoothly. Thus, as the **Iron Age I** opens, we find our Israelite settlers up in the central hill country. They are fully engaged in the task of transforming the heavily wooded hillsides into farmland, terracing those hillsides to hang on to their topsoil, and establishing hundreds of new Iron I villages along the spine of the "hill country of the Amorites" (Deut 1:7, 19, 20), north and south of the Jezreel Valley. There is no question that the Israelites have arrived. But as Deborah's drama will remind us, if the Israelites are going to *control* Canaan, they've got a lot more territory they need to control—and they aren't going to be able to dodge the coasts and the Jezreel Valley forever.

---

apiru (Ugaritic)—social status of people who were variously described as rebels, outlaws, raiders, mercenaries, bowmen, servants, slaves, and laborers

Ugaritic—extinct Northwest Semitic language; Amorite language

central hill country—geographic region between coastal plain and Jordan River Valley

---

First Contact

Do you remember the sunset scene early on in the film *Gone with the Wind?* The Civil War has not yet begun, and the beautiful (but indulged) Scarlett O'Hara is (once again) caught up in her own childish causes. Her immigrant father, Gerald O'Hara, will have none of it. He speaks of Tara—their family estate—and reminds Scarlett that she will one day inherit that land and how that is all that really matters. "I don't want it! Plantations don't mean anything!" she pouts. Her father's response is fierce: "Do you mean to tell me, Katie Scarlett O'Hara, that Tara, that *land* doesn't mean anything to you? Why, land is the only thing in the world worth workin' for, worth fightin' for, worth dyin' for, because it's the only thing that lasts!" She accuses him of talking "like an Irishman." And of course anyone who has lingered over "Danny Boy" or Yeats's "The Lake Isle of Innisfree" knows it's true—he *is* talking like an Irishman. Because the Irish love their land. And this father knows that the same love lies deep in the heart of his impish child: "To anyone with a drop of Irish blood in them, why, the land they live on is like their mother," he declares. "It'll come to you, this love of the land, there's no getting away from it if you're Irish." Can I say the same was true for the Israelites? The land—in all its beauty, drama, ferocity, and danger—was their hope, their sustenance, their very identity. And they loved every inch of it.

Into the Book

In our study, you will hear the words "territory," "tribal allotments," and "land" over and over again. Why is that? Because in God's great plan of redemption, getting the people of God (Israel) into the place of God (Canaan) so that their families and farms could flourish in a space safe from their enemies and graced by God's presence in the tabernacle was an essential part of the plan. Thus, the promise of land is an essential part of the plan as well. Let's take a look.

Turn in your Bible and read **Genesis 11:26–32**.

- Who are the characters in this very early story of the people of God? List their names here.

- You likely know "Abram" as "Abraham." God changes his name in Genesis 17. What do you know about Abraham?

- Abraham is called the "Father of the Jews." What do you think this means?

- What is Abram and Sarai's great problem (v. 30)?

Next read **Genesis 12:1–9**. This is Abram's first covenant encounter with Yahweh.

---

covenant—Hebrew בְּרִית *běrît*, from a root with the sense of "cutting"; covenants were made by passing between cut pieces of flesh of an animal sacrifice. Two types of covenants are in the Bible, the obligatory and promissory.

• The list of characters has now narrowed. Write the names in a list here.

• List the promises that God offers Abram in verses 1–3 here.

• In your response to the previous question, underline the promise that involves land (vv. 1, 6).

• What must Abram do to receive these promises?

• How many times does the word "land" appear in verses 1–9?

• We know from the previous passage that *one* of Abram and Sarai's great problems is the need for a child. Now that they have left their homeland, what is their other "great" need?

Now read **Genesis 15:1–21**. This is Abram's second covenant encounter with Yahweh.

- The cast of characters in this second covenant encounter has narrowed again. List the characters found in this encounter here.

- Write down the promises that God offers Abram.

- Write down what God offers Abram in verse 7.

- Describe Abram's response to God. Does Abram believe him?

- How does God seal his promise to Abraham?

- How many times does the word "land" appear in this passage?

Now jump to **Exodus 33:1–2**, a passage that immediately follows Moses's deliverance of the Israelites from Egypt. Do you recognize anything here from the promises to Abraham? Jot down three points of overlap.

1.

2.

3.

Now turn to **Deuteronomy 6:10–15**, a passage from Moses's last words to the Israelites just after the wilderness wanderings have concluded and just before they enter Canaan. Jot down three points of overlap that you recognize from the promises to Abraham.

1.

2.

3.

Finally, read **Joshua 1:1–9**, Joshua's first words to the Israelites after Moses hands over the reins. Do you hear it again?

- Name two things in this passage that Yahweh first promised to Abraham.
  1.

  2.

- What must Israel do and be to succeed in their mission? Jot down two things here.
  1.

  2.

Real People, Real Places, Real Faith

As you have learned, the promise of land, specifically the land of Canaan, was essential to God's covenant with his people—first identified with Abraham, reiterated to Moses, and declared under Joshua. There's no getting around it: If the children of Abraham were going to become a "great nation" (Gen 12:2), if "all the families of the earth" were going to be blessed by God's choosing of Abraham (Gen 12:3 NASB), and if a Messiah was going to be born for all people . . . Canaan would have to be conquered (Gen 15:7). Indeed, the entire story of Israel's oppression in Egypt and the great deliverance of the exodus finds its culmination in this one great promise of land. So when Joshua leads the tribes across the Jordan, he knows exactly what his job is: to be "strong and very courageous" (Josh 1:7) so that the plan of God and the kingdom of God can move forward and Israel might claim its inheritance. But as we learned in our first video, Joshua will not be able to finish the task alone. Yes, Joshua broke the back of Canaanite power and established a foothold in the land. But the tribes will have to expand that foothold to fully possess their inherited territories themselves. Check it out: Our book of Judges opens (1:1) with the question, "Who of us is to go up first to fight against the Canaanites?" What we find in the story of Israel's conquest and settlement is that *each citizen* of the kingdom of God we know as Israel will have to throw their shoulder behind this wheel. *Everyone* is going to have to join this mission—or this mission isn't going to happen.

Our People, Our Places, Our Faith

Have you ever found yourself thinking that it's the pastor's job to build the kingdom of God in your community? You know, "We hire people for that!" Or perhaps you've understood that your pastoral leadership needs your help, but you've thought, "Yeah, that's not my gifting." So you've found yourself sitting on the sidelines, perhaps comfortable with the fact that no one at work or school really knows you as a churchgoer or a Christian. Or maybe you've been an active servant in your church's community ministry, but right now, well, you're just tired. Transport yourself back into Israel's world for a moment. Imagine how you might feel if you were an Iron Age Israelite sitting on the front porch of your newly constructed four-room, pillared house, looking out across the Jezreel Valley. You might be thinking about how hard the journey has been and how grateful you are that the conquest is over. You might be super excited about your new house and focused on getting that perimeter wall built to help protect your expanding flocks. You might be crunching numbers in your head about the profit this year's barley crop is going to bring in and excited about the new baby on the way. You smile when you think about how you and your clan stood and fought with Joshua. "Man, we did good!" And how you hung in there until the Canaanites were routed. "Good job, team!" But then you think about the *other* territory that belongs to your clan that your tribe just hasn't gotten to yet, the land Joshua said you were still responsible to fight for. Your smile fades. "Really? That land too? Can't we be done now? My family is comfortable, the farm is good, the neighbors like me, and I'm having a great time down at the Canaanite country club. Do I really need to do *more*?"

Day 2: Maps, Maps, Maps

First Contact

Do you remember the Tom Hanks and Meg Ryan classic *Sleepless in Seattle*? Some among us can quote every line! There is a scene in the film where Annie (Meg Ryan), having flown from Baltimore to Seattle to meet Sam (Tom Hanks), is driving in her rental car. She is new to Seattle, and GPS isn't a thing yet. So, to the audience's amusement, Annie finds herself in the middle of traffic, wrestling with a huge paper map that is doing more to block the windshield than to get her where she's going. Can anyone relate? The GPS on our phones makes navigating traffic far easier, and I'm grateful. But when it comes to getting the big picture—planning a cross-country trip or plotting out exactly where you're going to buy a new house—there is nothing like a big, old-fashioned, paper map to put it all in perspective. Anyone with me?

Into the Book

In the video for session 1, you saw a map of the tribal allotments promised to the twelve tribes. We've also placed that map at the beginning of each session's individual study for your reference. Familiarize yourself with the locations of the tribal territories, as we will refer to them often.

Now take a look at **Joshua 21:43–45** (here and throughout, boldface is my own).

43 So the LORD gave Israel all the land he had sworn to give their ancestors, and **they took possession of it and settled there.** 44 The LORD gave them rest on every side, just as he had sworn to their ancestors. Not one of their enemies withstood them; the LORD gave all their enemies into their hands. 45 Not one of all the LORD's good promises to Israel failed; every one was fulfilled.

One would think reading this summary statement that all of Canaan had been conquered, the cities emptied, and the Canaanites completely driven out. But as we learned in our video, one would be wrong!

Take a look at Yahweh's words to Joshua in **Joshua 13:1–7**.

13:1 When Joshua had grown old, the LORD said to him, "You are now very old, and **there are still very large areas of land to be taken over.**

² "This is the land that remains: all the regions of the Philistines and Geshurites, ³ from the Shihor River on the east of Egypt to the territory of Ekron on the north, all of it counted as Canaanite though held by the five Philistine rulers in Gaza, Ashdod, Ashkelon, Gath and Ekron; the territory of the Avvites ⁴ on the south; all the land of the Canaanites, from Arah of the Sidonians as far as Aphek and the border of the Amorites; ⁵ the area of Byblos; and all Lebanon to the east, from Baal Gad below Mount Hermon to Lebo Hamath.

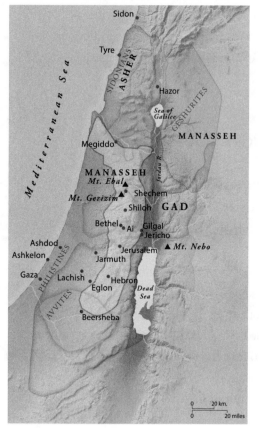

Israel's Conquered Land

⁶ "As for all the inhabitants of the mountain regions from Lebanon to Misrephoth Maim, that is, all the Sidonians, I myself will drive them out before the Israelites. **Be sure to allocate this land to Israel for an inheritance, as I have instructed you,** ⁷ and divide it as an inheritance among the nine tribes and half of the tribe of Manasseh."

What is the current state of Israel's possession of this territory according to this passage?

Let's look at another map. This one shows the physical surface, or topography, of the land of Israel. Notice that the land of Israel is made up of nearly ten topographical regions, each distinct from the other, ranging from steep mountains to deep valleys; from lush, green agricultural areas to dry, barren desert lands.[1] Some terms you'll hear throughout this study include the "hill country," "Negev," "foothills," and "Transjordan." Identifying all these regions is challenging, but as the geography of Canaan is the stage on which Deborah and Barak's story is told, we're going to have to roll up our sleeves and sort out the spaces that occupy this epic tale.

- First find and highlight the **Coastal Plain** on the map. With its many springs and access to the Mediterranean, this region is "prime real estate," and is therefore where many of the most formidable Canaanite city-states were located. Not only is this one of the most productive agricultural areas in the country, it is also home to the major north-south international highway introduced in the lecture: the **Via Maris**!

- Next, find and highlight the **Shephelah**, located between the coastal plain and the **Central Mountains** (commonly called the central hill country). The land of the Shephelah is excellent terrain for vineyards and olive yards.

- Highlight **Central Mountains** and write "Negev" just below Beersheba.

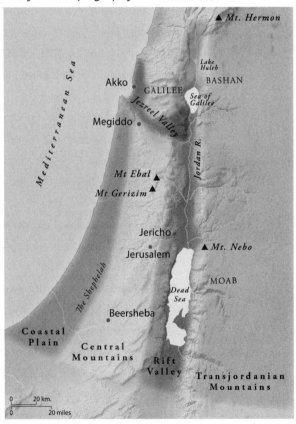

Physical Topography of Israel's Promised Land

---

1   See Amihai Mazar, *Archaeology of the Land of the Bible 10,000–586 B.C.E.* (New York: Doubleday, 1990), 1–9; and Carl G. Rasmussen, *Zondervan Atlas of the Bible* (Grand Rapids: Zondervan, 2010), 21–28; 33–35; 62–64.

Deborah's story begins in the central mountains. This topographical region stretches from northern **Galilee** (near the city of Dan, just north of Lake Huleh on this map) all the way to the **Negev** (near the city of Beersheba). Forested in the early days of Israel's settlement, our "smallholder" Israelite farmers cleared and terraced this land to build their homesteads and farms. The land here is fertile, and the twenty to forty inches of annual rainfall produces crops of wheat and barley as well as olive trees and vineyards. But the land is *rugged!* Clearing it was immensely labor intensive. The deep V-shaped valleys made travel very difficult and served to isolate this territory from much of the rest of Canaan. The hill country is where we find the tribal territory of **Naphtali** (Barak's tribe) and the **Benjamin Plateau** that houses the palm of Deborah. Look back at the conquered land map to refresh your memory of these locations. Keep in mind that this hill country was where Israel's initial settlement occurred.

- Next, find and highlight the **Rift Valley** and **Jordan River** on the map. The valley runs the entire length of the promised land, from Dan to Beersheba (cf. Judg 20:1; 1 Sam 3:20; 2 Sam 3:10). Toward the north it is lush and green. The ancient city of **Hazor**, which will come into play later in our story, is in the Rift Valley, lying just southwest of Lake Huleh.

- Place a dot just southwest of Lake Huleh to indicate the city of **Hazor** and write "Hazor" on the map.

- Highlight the **Sea of Galilee**. This body of water is a beautiful freshwater reservoir and a major source of fish.

- Write "Arabah" just below **Rift Valley** on the map. The **Arabah**, with its rugged, rock-strewn terrain, very little vegetation, and fewer than two inches of rainfall annually, begins just south of the Dead Sea.

- Highlight **Transjordanian Mountains**. The Transjordan is also called "the east of Jordan," or as in some versions, "beyond the Jordan eastward." The northern border of the Transjordan is marked by the famous snow-capped **Mount Hermon**, and its southern border is the land of **Edom**. In between is the well-watered region of **Bashan**, rich with volcanic soil and known for its agriculture, and the land of **Moab**, where wheat and barley may be grown.

- Highlight **Jezreel Valley**. The valley is ideal for agriculture: full of deep, rich topsoil that has accumulated from centuries of wash coming down off the Galilean hillsides, graced with excellent rainfall (about twenty inches annually), abundant springs, and the modest but reliable **Kishon River**. The valley is also valuable because of its location. This valley is home to the only east-west pass through the hill country in Canaan. It is in the Jezreel Valley that the **Via Maris** crosses, connecting Mesopotamia to Egypt. And it is here where every caravan and army emerging from those two superpower civilizations will pass as well.

Name three reasons why the ancients would want to control the Jezreel Valley.

1.

2.

3.

Name three things you now know about the central hill country.

1.

2.

3.

Real People, Real Places, Real Faith

As you've seen and heard, when we reach the book of Judges, "there are still large areas of land to be taken" (Josh 13:1). In fact, we regularly bump into the words "but" or "yet" regarding the lands promised to the tribes. For example, in Joshua 13:13, "**But** the Israelites did not drive out the people of Geshur and Maakah"; Joshua 17:12–13, "**Yet** the Manassites were not able to occupy these towns. . . . They subjected the Canaanites to forced labor **but** did not drive them out completely." What we are hearing in these passages is that Israel has *begun* their mission of possessing the promised land, but they have a long way to go before they complete it. And as we've read, the only way the mission will be completed is if the Israelites put their confidence in the faithfulness of Yahweh *and obey the covenant*. In many ways Israel's situation is simple: obey the covenant, gain territory; disobey the covenant, lose territory. But as we are about to learn, *simple* is not *easy*. Israel will be constantly tempted by the world around them to worship the gods of Canaan, establish alliances that violate Yahweh's covenant, and grow complacent with what they already have. What is the great threat here? That Israel will choose the road of least resistance. That God's people will choose to assimilate to the culture around them rather than fulfilling their mission to *transform* the culture around them. That Israel will allow themselves to be conformed to the image of the Canaanites rather than conformed to the image of their God. Sound familiar?

Our People, Our Places, Our Faith

I have a dear friend whom my husband and I discipled in his younger years. Jim was (and is!) a delightful fellow. Warm, fun, funny, a talented musician, a guy who loved people and was always "all in" in every conversation. So much potential! So whenever we would meet to talk about his life and calling, I usually asked for more: more direction, more ambition, more self-discipline. Jim? Well, he found my enthusiasm for his future a bit baffling. His classic response? "Why do you want my life to be so perfect?" I love this line! And we laugh about it now nearly every time we get together. Where I saw Jim's gifts and his potential to make a huge impact for the kingdom, Jim was much more focused on being comfortable. People liked him; he was content; and although he wasn't making much money, he was making enough to pay the bills. So why did I want more for him? I wonder if that's how the conversation between Yahweh and the Israelites went in the days of the judges? Israel had achieved a foothold in the land. Their houses were built and farmland cleared. So although the resources available to them in the hill country were very limited and the best of their promised land was still in the hands of their oppressors, our heroes managed to convince themselves that partial possession of the promised land was enough. Yahweh disagreed.

Why did God want their lives to be so perfect?

Why does he want *our* lives to be so perfect?

Day 3:
Superheroes and Scoundrels

First Contact

Do you know the story of the gunfight at the O.K. Corral? The setting was the boomtown of Tombstone, Arizona, on the edge of the American Wild West. The confrontation was the result of a long-standing feud between the cow-rustling Cowboys (Billy Claiborne, Ike and Billy Clanton, and Tom and Frank McLaury) and local law enforcement, specifically town marshal Virgil Earp. There were few rules in this silver mining town on the edge of the American frontier. It was full of brothels and gambling and thievery and described by many as "an open range for outlaws." But Virgil Earp intended to change that. So, enlisting his two brothers Morgan and Wyatt (along with Doc Holliday), this US Marshal took his stand against the outlaws. The trials and newspaper clippings since have struggled to differentiate the good guys from the bad guys in this classic tale— who was armed and who wasn't, who shot first and who tried to lay down their arms. In sum, was this a tale of murder or self-defense? No one actually knows. Partly because in the liminal space of the American frontier there was often very little daylight between heroes and villains, lawmen and gangsters, superheroes and scoundrels. Both were larger than life; both "colored outside the lines." In the words of Harvey Specter—another guy who colors outside the lines—sometimes "good guys gotta do bad things to make the bad guys pay."[1] Welcome to the age of the judges.

Into the Book

The book of Joshua ends with Joshua's dramatic farewell speech and his exhortation to the Israelites to faithfully serve Yahweh so that they will succeed in possessing the land (24:19–33). The book of Judges opens with Israel's faithful response to this exhortation and re-rehearses

---

1   Harvey Specter, "Dog Fight," *Suits*, Season 1 Episode 12.

Joshua's timely death and burial in his own tribal territory (1:1–2:9). This overlap lets us know several things. One, that the biblical authors want us to understand the book of Judges as the sequel to the book of Joshua. Two, that whereas Joshua was the glue that held Israel's era of conquest together, he is now turning the next chapter of the story over to the tribes. And three, that the tribes are going to struggle without his leadership. This sets the stage for our unlikely heroes, the judges!

Joshua 24:14–18, 23–24

14 "Now fear the LORD and serve him with all faithfulness. Throw away the gods your ancestors worshiped beyond the Euphrates River and in Egypt, and serve the LORD. 15 But if serving the LORD seems undesirable to you, then choose for yourselves this day whom you will serve, whether the gods your ancestors served beyond the Euphrates, or the gods of the Amorites, in whose land you are living. But as for me and my household, we will serve the LORD."

16 Then the people answered, "Far be it from us to forsake the LORD to serve other gods! 17 It was the LORD our God himself who brought us and our parents up out of Egypt, from that land of slavery, and performed those great signs before our eyes. He protected us on our entire journey and among all the nations through which we traveled. 18 And the LORD drove out before us all the nations, including the Amorites, who lived in the land. We too will serve the LORD, because he is our God. . . ."

23 "Now then," said Joshua, "throw away the foreign gods that are among you and yield your hearts to the LORD, the God of Israel."

24 And the people said to Joshua, "We will serve the LORD our God and obey him."

- Joshua tells the Israelites what it will take for Israel to succeed in possessing the land. Highlight the answer found in verses 14–15 and 23.
- How do the people respond to Joshua's instructions? What reason do they give for their choice?

- Joshua begins and ends his instructions with the same command to "throw away" the gods of their ancestors and the gods of Canaan (vv. 14, 23). Why might this command be so important?

Now let's turn to the book of Judges. The book is made up of a **prologue** (1:1–2:4), twelve cycles of "**hero tales**" (3:7–16:31) and an **epilogue** (with appendixes, 17:1–21:25). It is in the twelve cycles that we meet our twelve judges. Each judge is a bit larger than life, and they get "larger" as they go! I will categorize them as exemplary, triumphant, ambivalent, or tragic. Our girl Deborah falls into the category of "triumphant." But to give you a chance to meet *all* the judges, the plan is for you to study one judge in depth every week in your day 4 studies. Here, you will briefly meet the entire cast of characters. The following passages indicate where each judge's narrative is found. Skim the passage in your Bible and fill in the chart. Note: In the longer stories, specific verse references are provided to help you locate the requested information. Note: Table key on p. 213.

Scripture passage in Judges	Name of the judge	The sin of the Israelites (if provided in the text)
1. 3:7–11		
2. 3:12–30		
3. 3:31		
4. 4:1–5:31		(4:1, 4)
5. 6:1–8:35	(6:11)	(6:1, 7–10)
6. 10:1–2 **7.** 10:3–5		
8. 10:6–12:7		(10:6–10, 13)
9. 12:8–10 **10.** 12:11–12 **11.** 12:13–15		
12. 13:1–16:31	(13:24–25)	

Real People, Real Places, Real Faith

Joshua's instructions to Israel were clear: If you want to take possession of this land, you have to keep the covenant. The most essential part of that covenant is also the most essential part of the Ten Commandments: "I am [Yahweh] your God. . . . You shall have no other gods before me" (Exod 20:2–3). Joshua had told them, "Fear [Yahweh] and serve him with all faithfulness. Throw away the gods your ancestors worshiped beyond the Euphrates River and in Egypt, and serve [Yahweh]" (Josh 24:14). The people's response to this directive was equally clear: "Far be it from us to forsake [Yahweh] to serve other gods!" (Josh 24:16). But as we will see, this sort of single-mindedness wasn't going to be as easy as everyone thought.

Why would it be so hard for Israel? When the tribes entered the land of Canaan under Joshua's leadership, they were moving into a land filled with many gods. The gods of Canaan were El, Baal, Asherah, Anat, Mot, Dagon, Chemosh, and Molech. Their temples and their festivals could be found on every high hill and in every grove of green trees. These gods were each represented by elaborate, lifelike statues that their worshipers dressed, fed, and housed in temples to make sure the gods were content. If the gods *weren't* content, well, bad things would happen. In the mind of the polytheist (one who worships multiple gods), the gods were territorially bound. Thus, the Canaanites believed that these gods *lived* in Canaan. So for Israel to immigrate into the territory and fail to honor these resident gods with offerings and worship was to put their families, flocks, and farms at risk. As Baal was the god of fertility and rain, and Asherah was the goddess of pregnancy and birth, to *not* honor this divine couple took a great deal of conviction (and courage)! How would our settling Israelites have the clarity of thought, the single-mindedness, to resist the worldview of their Canaanite neighbors? It is hard to swim upstream against the cultural tide.

Our People, Our Places, Our Faith

How does Israel's struggle against assimilating into the worship practices of Canaan help us understand our own journey of faith? Paul tells us in Romans 12:2, "Do not conform to the pattern of this world, but be transformed by the renewing of your mind. Then you will be able to test and approve what God's will is—his good, pleasing and perfect will." But as we have discussed, it is *hard* to swim upstream against the cultural tide! Doing so invites the title of "outlier," "difficult," or even "crazy person." As the anonymous quote goes, "When the whole world is running towards a cliff, he who is running in the opposite direction appears to have lost his mind." How hard it is to resist what our neighbors are convinced is true! And what a risk it is *not* to embrace our society's value system and worship their gods. Israel's story gives us a concrete image of what it means to be a "peculiar people" (I Pet 2:9 KJV) . . . "aliens and strangers" (I Pet 2:11 NASB 1995). Do we have to be *weird*? No. Do we have to be people of conviction and courage who are willing to be different? Yes.

What happens in your world when you don't embrace your group's value system?

What happens when you resist in word or deed what they find so important?

Day 4: Meet the Judges

Othniel

1

Othniel

Meaning of name: "God is my strength" or "God has helped me"

Family background: Son of Kenaz, Caleb's younger brother, tribe of Judah

Title given: Deliverer who saved Israel

Israel's disobedience: Forgot Yahweh, served the Baals and the Asherahs

Empowerment: The Spirit of the Lord

Oppressor: Cushan-Rishathaim, king of Aram

Length of oppression: Eight years

Length of peace: Forty years

First Contact

Every emerging nation has a heroic past, a time when the task of survival is still foremost such that the regular running rules of civilized living are often sidelined and larger-than-life sword (or pistol)- swinging heroes wind up center stage. This is the story of Virgil and Wyatt Earp. It is also the story of the book of Judges. Lawson Stone says it like this: "Like all heroic literature, these stories celebrate the exploits of an outstanding individual. No eulogizing of the ordinary here, no democracy of the mediocre. Physicality becomes the idiom of excellence. Whether handsome or ugly, heroes are never common."[1]

As noted in the introduction, on each of the day 4 studies, we will introduce you to one of Deborah's colleagues in the book of Judges. As you read and learn about each judge, find and circle their name on the following map.

This week's study focuses on Othniel. Although he is rarely named in sermons, this man is universally recognized as *the* exemplar of what a judge should be. He was Israel's *first* judge—and became a model for those to come. Othniel hails from the tribe of Judah (Josh 15:13–19). His name means "God is my strength" or "God has helped me."[2]

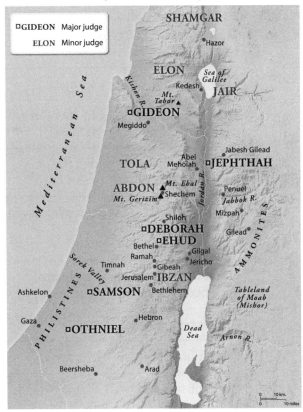

Map of Israel's Judges

---

1   Lawson G. Stone, *Judges*, Cornerstone Biblical Commentary, vol. 3 (Carol Stream, IL: Tyndale, 2012), 197–98.

2   Jack M. Sasson, *Judges 1–12: A New Translation with Introduction and Commentary*, Anchor Yale Bible Commentaries (New Haven: Yale University Press, 2014), 146.

Reading & Observing

Othniel's story is found in **Judges 3:7–11**.

As Othniel is the model for the judges to follow, his account includes all the information that we discovered in the description of the judges cycle. This chart can help as you read his story. Use the space provided to note additional details.

Cycle found in Judges 2:11–19	Othniel (Judges 3:7–11)
Israelites did evil in the eyes of the Lord	3:7
They served other gods, forsook the Lord	3:7 Baals and Asherahs
They aroused the Lord's anger	3:8
The Lord gave them/sold them into the hands of raiders/enemies	3:8
The people groaned under the oppression; cried out to the Lord	3:9
The Lord raised up judges who saved them	3:9 Othniel is called "a deliverer" instead of judge
When the judge died, the people returned to following other gods	3:12
Oppressor	3:8
Length of peace	3:11
Other observations	3:10 "The Spirit of the LORD came on him"
Death notice	3:11

Responding: What's Your Territory?

Each week, we will revisit the three questions posed in the video. As God begins to speak to you through this study, use the following space as a type of journal to track your journey with these questions.

In this week's individual lesson, we explored the land that the Israelites were commanded to conquer. We looked at the promise that began with Abraham. We identified the tribal territories and saw for ourselves how much was still left to be done even after the "conquest" was complete. And we saw how the Israelites struggled with the temptation to conform to their surroundings rather than living into their role to be God's agent of transformation. So as we come to the end of this session, let's ponder our questions again:

- What territory can you see from where you're standing that belongs to the kingdom of God and, for whatever reason, is not yet in the hands of God's people?

- Is it worth fighting for?

- What are you going to do about it?

SESSION 2

Arriving and Obeying Are Not the Same Thing

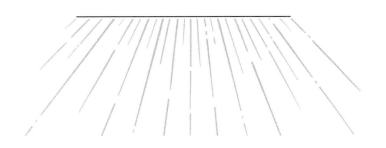

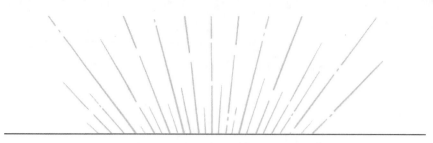

SESSION 2: GROUP MEETING

Schedule

GROUP MEETING
Session 2 Video Teaching and Discussion

INDIVIDUAL STUDY
Day 1: How Did We Get Here?

Day 2: How Do We Get Out of Here?

Day 3: Who Will Lead Us?

Day 4: Meet the Judges—Ehud

Getting Started

Leader, open your group by first asking if there are any questions regarding the homework. Then ask these icebreaker questions.

- Tell the group the first thing that comes to your mind when you think about America's Wild West.
- Do you have a favorite Western? Who was your favorite character and why? Was your favorite character a little "edgy"?
- Without looking in your Bibles or your homework, tell the group the name of the judge you learned about in the individual study, and share one thing you learned about them. Any "edginess" there?

Watch Session 2 Video:
Arriving and Obeying Are Not the Same Thing
[29 Minutes]

Streaming video access instructions are on the inside front cover of each study guide.

Video Outline

Follow along during the video, take notes, or write down questions and aha moments as you like.

I. The arrival of Israel in Canaan and an archaeological moment with me!

    A. New settlement pattern

    B. New architecture

    C. New agricultural methods

    D. New pottery

    E. New taboos

II. The era of the judges

    A. Israel's heroic past

        1. The task of survival is foremost

        2. Regular rules do not apply

    B. Era of liminal space

        1. "Liminal" comes from Latin *limen*, meaning "threshold"

        2. The space between what Israel was (a tribal confederation) and what Israel was becoming (a monarchy)

III. The structure of the book of Judges

    A. Twelve heroic tales

B. A twelve-tier cycle

IV. The theological point in Israel's covenant

    A. Obedience results in national security

    B. Disobedience results in national insecurity

V. The book map

    A. One chapter of prologue

    B. Twelve tales of twelve heroes

    C. Three chapters of epilogue

VI. The collapse of a community

    A. The narrative or story of Judges 19

    B. The point Judges 19 makes about the covenant people? "Everyone did as they saw fit" (Judg 17:6; 21:25)

    C. The end result?

1. Rather than winning new territory, the Israelites are losing territory

2. Rather than transforming Canaanite culture, they are being transformed by it

Dialogue, Digest & Do

Discuss the following as a group.

• How has the description of the period of the judges as the "Wild West" affected your understanding of the settlement period in Israelite history? What modern-day connection do you make to their circumstance or situation?

• Have a volunteer read **Romans 12:2** aloud to the group. Now that you know about Israel's struggle against assimilating into the worship practices of Canaan, in what ways can you relate more deeply to Paul's command against "conforming to the world"? What did you learn about the Canaanites and their worship practices in the video that demonstrates that their moral code was not the moral code of the God of Israel? Who are the Canaanites in your current context and what is the difference in moral codes you see around you today?

• Discuss some ways you have observed or see opportunity for the church to transform culture rather than be transformed by it. *Leader, this could be a divisive question. Use your good wisdom in shaping this question and the conversation!*

• What are some positive ways you can strengthen and share kingdom values in your current territory of influence?

Next Week

Before next week's group meeting, do your best to work your way through the four days of the session 2 individual study. In these individual studies we'll ask and answer the following: How did we get here? How do we get out of here? Who is going to lead us?

In the next group session, you'll hear words like "assimilation," "transformation," "third generation phenomenon," and "revival."

Closing Prayer

Leader, ask your group members if there is anything they would like prayer for, especially something highlighted by this week's video.

Israel's Promised Tribal Allotments

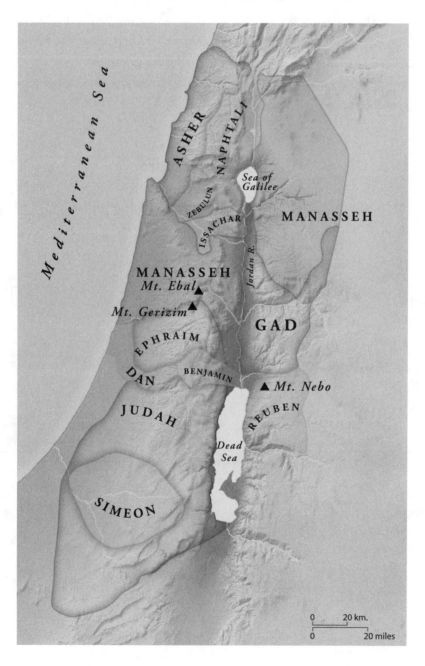

SESSION 2: INDIVIDUAL STUDY

The Cycle of the Judges

The lessons found in the individual studies focus on the *upcoming* week's video teaching.

A Word from Sandy

This week's study is all about cycles: cycles that are good—birth, growth, and maturity; cycles that are bad—stagnation, deterioration, and death; cycles that should be celebrated; and cycles that need to be broken. Our focus will be on the twelve cycles of the book of Judges, each of which revolves around one of the twelve heroes celebrated in the book. And in each we will see that all too familiar pattern of disobedience on the part of God's people that leads to foreign oppression and demands a hero. Were there only twelve judges in Israel's settlement period? No. There were surely many more, perhaps even more than one judge ruling at the same time in different regions of the country. But the twelve of the book of Judges are chosen as exemplars. Some are integrous and courageous, some are edgy, and a few are *so* edgy that we're still not sure if they were "good guys" or "bad guys"! A look at the "Judges map" in last week's lesson 4 shows that our biblical narrator has also chosen one judge from each of the regions of the promised land. In sum, we have twelve judges, one from each sector of Canaan, selected to tell the single story of God's people during this liminal era of redemptive history. Will Israel succeed in controlling the land promised since Abraham? Or will they fail?

Day 1: How Did We Get Here?

Real Time & Space

During the tribal confederation, the tribes lived independent lives. The only activities they regularly shared were their joint defense of the promised land and their united worship of Yahweh at the tabernacle. Thus, outside of the three pilgrim festivals and the periodic (and typically regional) call to arms, the tribes did not see each other much. The tribal sheiks handled local problems, and there was no centralized government, no taxation, no joint building projects, and no standing army. And they liked it that way. They saw Yahweh as their king, and their tribal elders as his local officials. The prophets and the judges were Yahweh's most influential representatives and, in combination with the priesthood housed at the tabernacle, his only national officers. The primary interest of each individual tribe was regional peace and prosperity and wrestling their allotted territory away from the Canaanites and Philistines.

In this early stage of Israel's history, Yahweh makes it clear that national success would be dependent on adherence to the covenant. The promise was that when Israel kept the covenant, they would experience prosperity and security. When they failed to keep the covenant, the nation would be disciplined by means of some sort of national disaster—typically foreign oppression. Keep clearly in your mind that Israel was a *theocracy*, so the citizens of this nation were the people of God, and the citizens of other nations were not. Moreover, the political and economic well-being of the nation was a direct reflection of whether God was pleased with his people. And because the people of God during this era of redemptive history were not terribly different from the people of God during our era of redemptive history, obedience to the covenant wasn't always a priority.[1]

---

1   Sandra L. Richter, *The Epic of Eden: A Christian Entry into the Old Testament* (Downers Grove, IL: IVP Academic, 2008), 191–92.

First Contact

You've heard it a thousand times. Perhaps you're the one who has said it a thousand times. "I'll do better next time." Or "I promise, this is the last time." Then when "the next (last) time" comes, the end result is the same. And with each "next time," the result (and behavior) grows more entrenched—and more destructive. One day we wake up with the broken pieces on the floor, and in disbelief we say, "How in the world did I get here?"

Into the Book

Judges 2:6–23 provides a summary of the Israelites' destructive cycle. Read the passage in your Bible, fill in the appropriate title for each of the stages using the following diagram, and answer the questions as you go. (Stage 1 has been done as an example.)

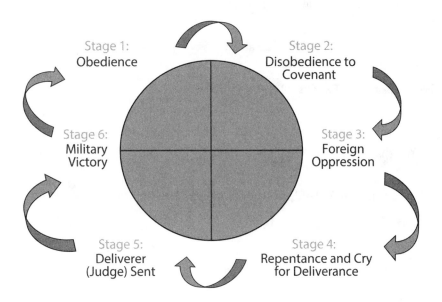

1. Stage 1 (v. 7):   *obedience*

2. What kind of experience with the Lord do verses 6–7 describe "the people" having?

3. Stage 2 (vv. 10–13):

4. How does verse 10 describe the experience of the next generation with the Lord?

5. List the ways that the Israelites "did evil in the eyes of the LORD":

6. Stage 3 (vv. 14–15):

7. Stage 4 (vv. 15b; 18b):

8. Stage 5 (v. 16a):

9. Stage 6 (vv. 16b; 18a):

10. What do you notice about the length of time the peace lasted?

11. What happened when the judge died?

12. What do you notice in verse 19 about the corruption of the Israelites?

13. What do verses 20–23 tell you about this point in the cycle?

Take a look now at **Exodus 20:2–3**.

I am the LORD your God, who brought you out of Egypt, out of the land of slavery.
    You shall have no other gods before me.

- Compare **Judges 2:11–13, 17–18** with **Exodus 20:2–3**.

Read **Joshua 23:12–13**.

¹² But if you turn away and ally yourselves with the survivors of these nations that remain among you and if you intermarry with them and associate with them, ¹³ then you may be sure that the LORD your God will no longer drive out these nations before you. Instead, they will become snares and traps for you, whips on your backs and thorns in your eyes, until you perish from this good land, which the LORD your God has given you.

• Underline the things that Joshua warns the Israelites against in verse 12.

Real People, Real Places, Real Faith

The narrator concludes Judges 2 by informing the reader that the Lord left the nations that remained after Joshua's death to "test Israel and see whether they [would] keep the way of the LORD and walk in it as their ancestors did" (v. 22). And again in 3:4 we read that the other nations were there to "test the Israelites to see whether they would obey the LORD's commands, which he had given their ancestors through Moses." What we see here is a whole generation of Israelites who do not know Yahweh, who had not seen Yahweh fight on their behalf. In 3:5–6 we find that this generation fails in three ways: (1) they were satisfied to live among the other nations rather than driving them out; (2) they intermarried with them, joining the community of faith to the community of Canaan; and (3) as a result they served the gods of Canaan: Baal, Asherah, Molech, and Dagon. How did they get there? In the words of Lawson Stone, "Israel frittered away its inheritance a little bit at a time. . . . Before settling for something *other than* Yahweh's covenant promises, Israel settled for something *less than* Yahweh's covenant promises."[2]

---

2   Lawson G. Stone, *Judges*, Cornerstone Biblical Commentary, vol. 3 (Carol Stream, IL: Tyndale, 2012), 222.

Our People, Our Places, Our Faith

In this lesson we have learned that after Joshua's successes, it was now the tribes' turn to pick up the mantle of leadership and fully *possess* the land. We've also seen that if this new generation would keep the covenant, and fight for the kingdom, then they too would see the mighty hand of God in action and would relaunch the cycle of faithfulness and revival among their people. The lesson to be learned here? *Each* generation needs to know their God, each needs to keep the covenant, and each needs to step out in faith so that Yahweh can fight on their behalf. In our next lesson we will compare Israel's cycle with that of the church.

So we want to start asking ourselves, In our real time and space, how are *we* forgetting the covenant?

How is it that we are neglecting *our* roles of leadership in fighting for the kingdom?

Is it time for revival in your community?

Day 2: How Do We Get Out of Here?

First Contact

Even though I am a complete coward when it comes to horror films, I have to admit that I am intrigued by the whole "monster in the closet" motif. How many times have you sat in your family room, watching the standard trope of the mysterious cabin/basement/closet pass over your television screen, and everyone in the room screams, "Don't go in there!" But do they listen? Nope. Even though they *know* that the closet has devoured the first six characters of the movie. Even though they are completely clear that something supernatural and nasty is going on in there. For some absurd reason these ill-fated movie stars are completely convinced that the closet won't get *them*. What is with that? Are they just stupid? Or is it that these characters think that they are somehow the exceptions to the power of the closet?

Into the Book

In our video lesson and yesterday's study, we saw how the Israelites ended up where they were. They went into the closet and became more corrupt than their ancestors (2:19). Thus, the question of the hour becomes: How do they get *out* of the closet?

We'll start with taking another close look at **Judges 2:16, 18–19**. Read the verses here, and answer the following questions.

¹⁶ Then the LORD raised up judges, who saved them out of the hands of these raiders. . . . ¹⁸ Whenever the LORD raised up a judge for them, he was with the judge and saved them out of the hands of their enemies as long as the judge lived; for the LORD relented because of their groaning under those who oppressed and afflicted them. ¹⁹ But when the judge died, the people returned to ways even

more corrupt than those of their ancestors, following other gods and serving and worshiping them. They refused to give up their evil practices and stubborn ways.

• What caused the Lord to relent?

• Look at verse 18 in at least three other translations. How do those versions render what the NIV translates "relented"?

• How was the judge empowered? What did the judge do?

• How long did the salvation from the enemy last (v. 19)?

Read **Joshua 23:6–8**.

⁶ Be very strong; be careful to obey all that is written in the Book of the Law of Moses, without turning aside to the right or to the left. ⁷ Do not associate with these nations that remain among you; do not invoke the names of their gods or swear by them. You must not serve them or bow down to them. ⁸ But you are to hold fast to the LORD your God, as you have until now.

• Underline each of the commands Joshua gives the Israelites. What is he calling them to?

Read **Judges 2:20–21**. You've already seen these verses, but let's look at them again. In the verse prior to this, the narrator tells the reader that as soon as the judge died, the people went right back to serving gods other than Yahweh.

> [20] Therefore the LORD was very angry with Israel and said, "Because this nation has violated the covenant I ordained for their ancestors and has not listened to me, [21] I will no longer drive out before them any of the nations Joshua left when he died.

- Why will Yahweh no longer drive out the nations?

- What then does this tell you about how they get out of where they are?

Real People, Real Places, Real Faith

Imagine you're an Israelite living during the time of the judges. Imagine you're one of those families who has been "shattered and crushed" by *eighteen years* of military and economic oppression at the hands of the Philistines and Ammonites (Judges 10:6–10). Or maybe you're one of those families who have had to flee your family farm to shelter in the caves in the mountains to stay alive while the Midianites and Amalekites plunder your crops and herds (6:1–6). You cry out to the Lord for relief. Fervent prayers are prayed. And you are overjoyed when in response Yahweh sends a judge who steps up, musters the troops, and rescues you and your children from this impossible situation! But then it happens again. And again. Why does this keep happening? Maybe we need a better army. Maybe we should find a way to negotiate a treaty with the Canaanites. Or *maybe* there is something we're missing about our God and his promises regarding the promised land. Bingo. Joshua 1:7–9 says it best. The solution is simple: keep the covenant!

Our People, Our Places, Our Faith

So as we step back into *our* space, what territory are *we* the church letting slip through our fingers? Why do you think that is? Is it because we haven't remodeled our sanctuary according to what the consultants said would offer a more contemporary space for newcomers? Is it because we haven't rallied our people to vote for our chosen political party? Or is it our pastor's fault? Or might it be . . . *us*?

Ponder the words of our covenant Lord for a moment: "If you love me, keep my commands" (John 14:15).

Meditate on the truth of these words: "I am the true vine, and my Father is the gardener. He cuts off every branch in me that bears no fruit, while every branch that does bear fruit he prunes so that it will be even more fruitful. You are already clean because of the word I have spoken to you. Remain in me, as I also remain in you. No branch can bear fruit by itself; it must remain in the vine. Neither can you bear fruit unless you remain in me" (John 15:1–4).

Day 3: Who Will Lead Us?

First Contact

Todd Beamer. Do you recognize that name? Those of us who lived through 9/11 do. And any student who has walked through the Todd M. Beamer Student Center at Wheaton College remembers him as well. He was aboard United Airlines flight 93, one of four planes hijacked that horrible day. When Beamer recognized that his flight was about to be used as a weapon, targeting our nation's capital and untold numbers of civilians, he took action. Beamer and his courageous allies, Mark Bingham, Tom Burnett, and Jeremy Glick, were just regular folk. Todd was headed to a business meeting in California. He had a pregnant wife and two toddlers at home. All four men knew the risks. And every hero on that plane knew that if they took the action required, they had no chance of survival. But they said yes anyway. They forged a plan, called their loved ones, prayed the Lord's Prayer (and Psalm 23), and they rushed the cockpit. The rest is history. As President Bush stated in his memorial speech, "Some of our greatest moments have been acts of courage for which no one could have been prepared."[1]

Into the Book

Who will lead the Israelites? That is the question. Let's look at a few characters that Yahweh called to lead, or judge, Israel. Read the following passages and answer the questions after each.

Judges 3:9–10

> [9] But when they cried out to the LORD, he raised up for them a deliverer, Othniel son of Kenaz, Caleb's younger brother, who saved them. [10] The Spirit of the LORD came on him, so that he became Israel's judge and went to war.

---

1   George W. Bush, "Transcript of Bush Speech in Atlanta," CNN.com, November 8, 2011, http://edition.cnn.com /2001/US/11/08/rec.bush.transcript/.

- What is the reason that "the Spirit of the Lord came on [Othniel]"?

Judges 6:12, 14–16, 34

[12] When the angel of the Lord appeared to Gideon, he said, "The Lord is with you, mighty warrior."

[14] The Lord turned to him and said, "Go in the strength you have and save Israel out of Midian's hand. Am I not sending you?"

[15] "Pardon me, my lord," Gideon replied, "but how can I save Israel? My clan is the weakest in Manasseh, and I am the least in my family."

[16] The Lord answered, "I will be with you, and you will strike down all the Midianites, leaving none alive."

[34] Then the Spirit of the Lord came on Gideon.

- How does the Lord address Gideon in verse 12? What assurance does he give Gideon?

- What assignment does Yahweh give Gideon?

Judges 11:1, 29

[1] Jephthah the Gileadite was a mighty warrior. His father was Gilead; his mother was a prostitute.

[29] Then the Spirit of the Lord came on Jephthah.

- From the information given in verse 1, how do you think Jephthah fit into Israelite society?

- But yet, look at verse 29. How was he called?

Judges 13:2–3, 5, 24–25; 15:14

2 A certain man of Zorah, named Manoah, from the clan of the Danites, had a wife who was childless, unable to give birth. 3 The angel of the LORD appeared to her and said, "You are barren and childless, but you are going to become pregnant and give birth to a son. . . . 5 The boy is to be a Nazirite, dedicated to God from the womb."

24 The woman gave birth to a boy and named him Samson. He grew and the LORD blessed him, 25 and the Spirit of the LORD began to stir him while he was in Mahaneh Dan, between Zorah and Eshtaol.

15:14 As he approached Lehi, the Philistines came toward him shouting. The Spirit of the LORD came powerfully upon him. The ropes on his arms became like charred flax, and the bindings dropped from his hands.

- What does the angel of the Lord promise Manoah's wife?

- One phrase is repeated in each of the previous passages. Highlight the phrase that indicates where the judges received their empowerment for their tasks.

- Based on your observations, what conclusions do you make about who Yahweh calls to lead?

Real People, Real Places, Real Faith

In the New Testament, we see that God's modus operandi doesn't change. He continues to call on regular folk to lead the charge in building the kingdom. I am thinking about eleven undereducated, working-class guys standing on the side of an unnamed mountain in Galilee. They had accents—and not the kind you want. Everyone knew where they were from and mocked them for thinking that they had what it took to "play with the big boys." And yet the creator of the cosmos stands on that same unnamed mountain and entrusts these eleven with the kingdom. His command? "Get out there and make disciples! Go to every nation! Baptize them! Teach them the same stuff that I taught you!" Can you imagine the disciples' response? "Us? You think *we* can do this?" Then I think of the 120 people gathered in an upper room in Jerusalem praying on the day of Pentecost. As Paul describes the first converts in 1 Corinthians 1:26–27, few were wise in the world's eyes or powerful or wealthy. But they were called, and they did say yes. As a result, before the day was out, three thousand new converts were added to the kingdom (Acts 2:41)! How were these less-than-rockstars equipped for the seemingly impossible task ahead? "All of them were filled with the Holy Spirit and began to speak in other tongues as the Spirit enabled them" (Acts 2:4). I hope these New Testament passages remind you of Judges 3:10; 6:34; 15:14, where the Spirit came upon a regular guy or gal and transformed them into a superhero. This is the paradox of the kingdom: regular folk + the empowerment of the Holy Spirit = "*I will build my church*, and the *gates of Hades will* not overcome it" (Matt 16:18, emphasis mine).

Our People, Our Places, Our Faith

In each of the critical kingdom moments we have reviewed in this lesson—when the future of God's people and God's purposes hung in the balance—we hear the voice of Yahweh: "Have I not commanded you? Be strong and courageous. Do not be afraid; do not be discouraged, for the LORD your God will be with you wherever you go" (Josh 1:9). And because of the leadership of those who believed this message, the tide turned. The enemy was defeated. New territory was claimed. Were these emerging leaders superheroes? Categorically not. But because of their faith in the One who called, and the empowerment of the Spirit, the kingdom moved forward. Deborah and Barak's story is pushing us to ask if we are ready to be a part of that great story. Are we? I hope so! As Todd Beamer would say, "Okay. Let's roll."

Day 4: Meet the Judges

Ehud

2

Ehud

Meaning of name: Uncertain. Some suggestions include "my brother/father is Majesty" or "where is the majesty?"

Family background: Son of Gera, tribe of Benjamin

Title given: Deliverer

Israel's disobedience: They "did evil in the eyes of the LORD"

Oppressor: Eglon, king of Moab

Length of oppression: Eighteen years

Length of peace: Eighty years

Other information: He was "a left-handed man"; assassinated Eglon; struck down ten thousand Moabites

First Contact

Ehud is one of the most well-known judges in our book of heroes, likely because he is every inch the gunslinger's hero. Special agent or assassin? Hero or hooligan? Inquiring minds want to know! Often referred to as "the left-handed judge," Ehud uses his training as an elite warrior and his unexpected left-handed sword skills to take out Eglon, the king of Moab.

Ehud is from the tribe of Benjamin (1 Chr 7:6–12; 8:6; Judg 3:15). The meaning of Ehud's name is uncertain. Some suggestions include "my brother/father is Majesty" or "where is the majesty?"[1]

Reading & Observing

Ehud

Read **Judges 3:12–30**. Answer the following questions:

- Find **Ehud** on the map provided and circle his name.
- Circle the homeland of Eglon (look for **Tableland of . . .** east of the Jordan River).
- Circle the city that Eglon, the Ammonites, and the Amalekites conquered.
- What title is applied to Ehud in verse 15?

- Who did Ehud credit for the Israelites' victory over Moab (v. 28)?

Map of Israel's Judges

---

1   Sasson, *Judges*, 226.

Observe Ehud's life as judge in comparison to the cycle of the judges as you read.

Cycle found in Judges 2:11–19	Ehud (Judges 3:12–30)
Israelites did evil in the eyes of the Lord	3:12
They served other gods, forsook the Lord	
They aroused the Lord's anger	
The Lord gave them/sold them into the hands of raiders/enemies	3:12
The people groaned under the oppression, cried out to the Lord	3:15
The Lord raised up judges who saved them	3:15 "gave them a deliverer"
When the judge died, the people returned to following other gods	
Oppressor	3:12–13
Length of peace	3:30
Death notice	4:1

A bit more about Ehud and Eglon and that double-edged sword: As the story is typically told, Eglon is morbidly obese—think Star Wars and Jabba the Hutt. This tyrant is described as "an ineffectual 'fatted calf'" ready for slaughter at the hand of CIA superstar Ehud the Israelite.[2] They say that Eglon's girth is why Ehud's sword is "swallowed up" and can't be retrieved. Lawson Stone counters in his 2009 *Journal of Biblical Literature* article, "Eglon's Belly and Ehud's Blade." He argues that Eglon was not obese, but rather, like the bull-calf for which he was named, Eglon is actually a buff and totally *dangerous* warlord.[3] If so, then what about the sword and the fat? Stone identifies Ehud's homemade sword as a Naue II type sword, "a double-edged combat sword" that "would be long enough that its thrust would strike deeply

---

2   Lawson Stone, "Eglon's Belly and Ehud's Blade: A Reconsideration," *Journal of Biblical Literature* 128/4 (2009): 663.
3   Lawson G. Stone, *Judges*, Cornerstone Biblical Commentary, vol. 3 (Carol Stream, IL: Tyndale, 2012), 240; Stone, "Eglon's Belly and Ehud's Blade," 663.

and damage enough tissue to cause instantaneous, or at least very rapid, death."[4] And the fat closing over the sword (3:22)? When Ehud "plunged" (3:21) the sword into Eglon's belly, the thrust was so violent and deep that the hilt entered the king's body and the fat "of his abdomen enclosed around the grip."[5]

Responding: What's Your Territory?

In this week's individual lesson, we looked at how the Israelites ended up in the situation they were in: they failed to keep the covenant and followed after other gods. And we found the solution to getting out of that situation—a leader who would get them back on track with the covenant.

Now that you've learned more, let's ask those three questions again. Remember to use the space provided to track your growth as we progress in the study.

- What territory can you see from where you're standing that belongs to the kingdom of God and, for whatever reason, is not yet in the hands of God's people?

- Is it worth fighting for?

- What are you going to do about it?

---

4   Stone, *Judges*, 239–40.
5   Stone, *Judges*, 242.

SESSION 3

The Cycle of
the Judges

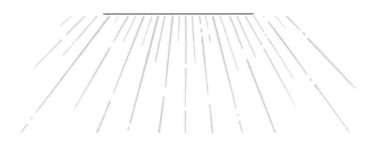

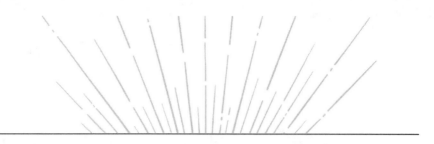

SESSION 3: GROUP MEETING

Schedule

GROUP MEETING

Session 3 Video Teaching and Discussion

INDIVIDUAL STUDY

Day 1: A Judge

Day 2: A Prophet

Day 3: An Arbitrator (and Her Tree)

Day 4: Meet the Judges—Gideon

Getting Started

Leader, open your group by first asking if there are any questions regarding the homework. Then ask these icebreaker questions.

- Tell the group the name of someone in your church/camp/institution's history who made a significant contribution in making your church/camp/institution what it was called to be. What was it they did? What did it cost them? What was the long-term impact of their leadership?

Watch Session 3 Video:
The Cycle of the Judges
[30 Minutes]

Streaming video access instructions are on the inside front cover of each study guide.

Video Outline

Follow along during the video, take notes, or write down questions and aha moments as you like.

I. How did we get here? (Judg 2:6–15; 3:5–6)

   A. Obedience (2:6–7)

      The people served the LORD throughout the lifetime of Joshua and of the elders who outlived him and who had seen all the great things the LORD had done for Israel. (v. 7)

   B. Disobedience (2:10–13)

After that whole generation had been gathered to their ancestors, another generation grew up who knew neither the LORD nor what he had done for Israel. (v. 10)

C. Oppression (2:14–15)

In his anger against Israel the LORD gave them into the hands of raiders who plundered them. He sold them into the hands of their enemies all around, whom they were no longer able to resist. (v. 14)

D. The third-generation phenomenon

1. First generation: those whose faith is their own

2. Second generation: those who have the influence of the first generation

3. Third generation: those who have no testimony to tell

E. Unfulfilled destiny (3:5–6)

How could the successors of Joshua, the heirs of the divine promise, lose their grip on that gift that stood as a goal and apex of the entire work of God narrated from the Creation through the Exodus experience to the conquest? The answer given in this carefully constructed and complex chapter is chilling: Israel frittered away its inheritance a little bit at a time. Before any claims of overt apostasy appear, the text impresses on the reader a process in which the nation simply compromised the divine purpose. Before settling for something *other than* Yahweh's covenant promises, Israel settled for something *less than* Yahweh's covenant promises.[1]

---

1   Lawson Stone, *Judges*, in Cornerstone Biblical Commentary, vol. 3 (Carol Stream, IL: Tyndale, 2012), 222.

II. How do we get out of here? (Judg 2:16–19)

    A. Judges (2:16)

        Then the LORD raised up judges, who saved them out of the hands of these raiders. (v. 16)

    B. Garth Rosell and the life cycle of the church; the cycle of revival

III. Who's going to lead us?

Dialogue, Digest & Do

Discuss the following as a group.

- Sandy speaks about the drifting Israelites as a generation whose faith was "not their own." How would you understand that phrase in modern culture today?

- What might be a comparative example you can think of today?

- Sandy says that "when the people of God have had no experience of God themselves, then we've got trouble." What do you think having an experience of God looks like? Can you name such an experience from your own life that you'd be willing to share? Where do we see trouble today when people of God have no such experiences to form them?

- Had you ever heard of the "life cycle of the church" before? Does the concept ring true for you?

- Have you ever been a part of a revival? Describe your experience to the group.

The Cycle of Revival

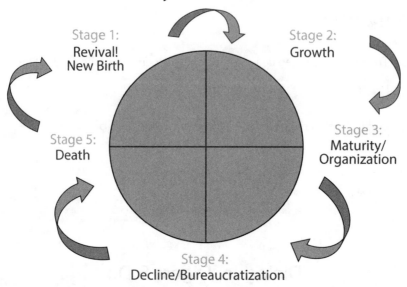

Stage 1:
**Revival!
New Birth**

Stage 2:
Growth

Stage 5:
Death

Stage 3:
**Maturity/
Organization**

Stage 4:
Decline/Bureaucratization

(Dr. Garth Rosell, Gordon Conwell Theology Seminary)

- Look at the cycle of revival chart here from the video.

- How is this cycle similar to the cycle of the judges? Where would you place your church/camp/denomination/organization on this chart?

- In the video, you heard the word "disruptors." Sandy speaks of them by several terms (one of which is "revivalist"). Can you name a disruptor from your own knowledge of the church's life?

Next Week

How are you doing on your homework? If you haven't been able to complete the four days of work yet, no worries. Complete all four of this week's studies. Next week we finally get to the part you've all been waiting for—meeting Deborah! We'll be looking at the functions of the judges, imagining what Deborah looked like, and learning a bit about trees in the Bible.

Closing Prayer

Leader, ask your group members if there is anything they would like prayer for, especially something highlighted by this week's video.

Israel's Promised Tribal Allotments

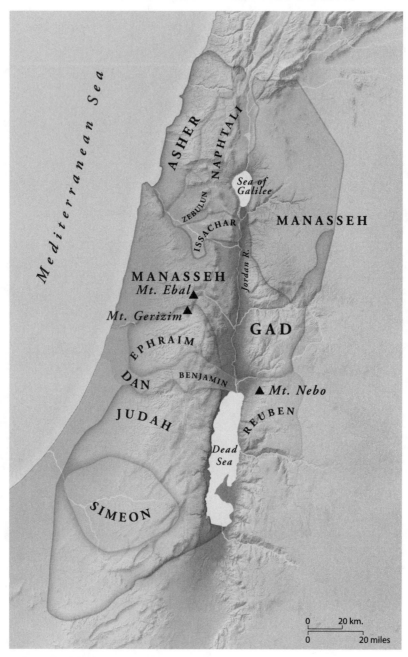

SESSION 3: INDIVIDUAL STUDY

Meet Deborah!

The lessons found in the individual studies focus on the *upcoming* week's video lecture.

A Word from Sandy

In our last study we began the conversation about "How do we get out of here?" In Israel's story, once they recognized that they had drifted off course—their God-given territory was slipping through their fingers—and the proverbial truck was now stuck in a proverbial ditch, they cried out for help. God answered their cry in the form of a Spirit-empowered leader who helped them face their opponents, win back their territory, and get that truck back on the road. What can we learn from Israel about getting back on course? Well, once again, the paradigmatic role of the "great story" comes to our aid. Just as Israel needed leaders, even unlikely leaders, the church needs the same. We need leaders, disruptors, and heroes who are willing to make the kingdom their first allegiance, stake their lives on the gospel, and unapologetically put the Great Commission back in the middle of the table.

So who is going to lead Israel? And who is going to lead us? I've got such good news! Because not only is our girl Deborah a leader with humility, integrity, and courage, she is also one of the most unlikely leaders of all time. As I say in the video, Deborah is not Wonder Woman. She has no exceptional biography. She is not of royal descent. She is not married to anyone famous; she is not Michelle Obama or Oprah Winfrey or even Barbara Bush. And yet she winds up leading Israel for more than forty years (and that in one of the most corrupt and chaotic eras of Israelite history). How did she wind up in that role? Pretty simple: She was called. And she said yes.

Day 1: A Judge

Real Time & Space

As I discuss at length in *The Epic of Eden: A Christian Entry into the Old Testament*,[1] ancient Israel's tribal society was very unlike contemporary Western, urban (or suburban) culture. With Israel being a traditional and tribal culture, family and kinship ties were the warp and weft (the foundation and fabric) of their society. There were no bureaucratic systems to administer legal or economic aid or provide a safety net for the marginalized. Rather, all ties to the legal and economic systems of Israel's world came through the family. In this world the individual was hardly recognizable; rather, the recognition of legal rights and responsibilities and societal agency were attributed to the individual family *unit*. And this was a family unit we would struggle to recognize. Rather than what we know as the "nuclear family," the typical family in Israel consisted of a patriarch (the oldest living male), his wife, his adult sons, their wives, their children, and any unmarried women. This extended family could include as many as three generations, up to twenty people plus whatever servants or clients the extended family had assimilated! For Abraham that was "318 trained men born in his household" (Gen 14:14)! These folk lived together on the family farm, practiced "diversified agriculture," and shared the labor and produce of their tribal inheritance. The family itself and their living space was known as the *bet ab* in Hebrew, "the father's household." Here the patriarch of the family exercised ultimate authority and likewise carried ultimate responsibility for the well-being of his household. He was the one to make the decisions, pass judgment, and steward the family for the next generation. Inheritance was transferred through the male line, and children always belonged to their fathers. Anthropologists speak of this system as "patrilineal." Thus, the family lived together in their shared space, interacted with society as a unit, and were buried together in multigenerational family tombs. As Marshall Sahlins stated in his classic work on the topic, the societal structure of patriarchal tribalism involves a "progressively inclusive series of groups" emanating from the patriarchal leaders: the *bet ab*, then the clan, then the tribe, and then the nation.[2]

---

1   Richter, *Epic of Eden: A Christian Entry into the Old Testament*, 25–37.
2   Marshall Sahlins, *Tribesmen: Foundations of Modern Anthropology* (Englewood Cliffs, NJ: Prentice Hall, 1968), 15.

Obviously this is not the structure of American or European society, and God is not asking us to mimic Israel's culture. But we *do* need to understand it. Why? Because understanding Israel's culture means we have a far better chance of understanding *them*. And once we understand *them*, we have a much better chance of understanding their encounter with their God.

So what about the women of Deborah's world? In Israel's patriarchal tribal culture, a woman's identity was defined by the men in her life. She was born her father's daughter, became her husband's wife, and, if she was lucky, aged into the esteemed role of her son's mother. Women were the mobile units in this society. A woman was the one who did the moving when a marriage occurred; she was the one who changed her tribal association. Her children were legally her husband's offspring, and any contact she had with the legal or economic systems happened through the men in her life. That is why your Bible is so concerned about widows and orphans—a woman without a father, husband, or adult son was a woman without advocacy or support. Our hero Deborah will be introduced to us, appropriately, as Lappidoth's wife. And we can assume she had children (Judg 5:7). But Deborah will *also* be introduced as military commander, tribal ruler, and theocratic prophet. In fact, those are the only roles our biblical narrator is interested in as he recounts her story. Why does that interest us? Because it is countercultural! I will often say in my teaching that "the gospel critiques every culture." And when we see the narrative of redemptive history swimming upstream against the surrounding culture, we want to ask why. Why is the narrator of the book of Judges focusing on this wife and mother as commander in chief? One answer is that this woman is a rockstar. Another answer, and applicable to us right now, the Holy Spirit has absolutely no qualms about defying societal norms to raise up and empower the people he needs to build his kingdom.

First Contact

The following list includes things that come to my mind when I hear the word "judge": A legal expert clothed in black, seated at a large wooden "bench," sporting a small ceremonial mallet known as a "gavel," elevated above the courtroom. You rise when they enter, you address them as "Your Honor," and they hold your fate in their hands. Powerful and intimidating for sure!

What I *don't* think about when I hear the word "judge" is Douglas MacArthur, Dwight D. Eisenhower, Stanley McChrystal. Nor do characters like William Wallace, Black Widow, James Bond, or Tony Stark spring to mind. But when we read the book of Judges, it is *exactly* the combination of these two types of characters that needs to take the stage. Seasoned steward of the covenant of Yahweh? Check. War-scarred military commander who would rather die than yield the territory to Israel's enemies? Check.

Into the Book

The word translated in our English Bibles as "judge" (or sometimes "leader"[3]) is a complex word indeed! It comes from the Hebrew root *shāpaṭ*, which has an entry in the standard scholar's Hebrew lexicon that extends for six pages! It has many cognates in surrounding languages (Akkadian, Amorite, Ugaritic, Aramaic, Arabic, and more!), and in each it has a mixed etymology. "To exercise authority" is one meaning; "the action that restores *shalom* to a community after it has been disturbed" is another.[4] In all these languages and cultures, the *shōpēṭ* is both ruler and judge, governor and arbitrator. And in each, interestingly, there are indicators that these are the characters who exercised leadership over their communities before a centralized government (a.k.a. a monarchy) emerged.

Deuteronomy 17:8–13

> [8] If cases come before your courts that are too difficult for you to judge—whether bloodshed, lawsuits or assaults—take them to the place the LORD your God will choose. [9] Go to the Levitical priests and to the judge who is in office at that time. Inquire of them and they will give you the verdict. [10] You must act according to the decisions they give you at the place the LORD will choose. Be careful to do everything they instruct you to do. [11] Act according to whatever they teach you and the decisions they give you. Do not turn aside from what they tell you, to the right or to the left. [12] Anyone who shows contempt for the judge or for the priest who stands ministering there to the LORD your God is to be put to death. You must purge the evil from Israel. [13] All the people will hear and be afraid, and will not be contemptuous again.

---

3 For example, see Judges 3:10, which supplies a footnote on the word "judge" suggesting an alternate translation of "leader." In other ancient texts outside the Old Testament, the term can also refer to an administrator of a district or a governor. See Ludwig Koehler and Walter Baumgartner, *The Hebrew and Aramaic Lexicon of the Old Testament* (*HALOT*) vol. 2 (Leiden: Brill, 2001), 1623–25. See also Stone, *Judges*, 188.

4 *HALOT* 2:1622; *HALOT* 2:1623.

- Why would cases be taken to a higher court (v. 8)?

- Who are those involved in the higher court (v. 9)? What is their responsibility?

- What are the responsibilities of the ones who brought the case to the higher court (vv. 10–11)? In these two verses, how many times are these individuals instructed to obey the higher court's decision?

- What is supposed to happen to "anyone who shows contempt"? Why?

- What function/role does the judge play in this scenario?

Let's look at another function of the judges. In Judges 6–8 Gideon is called on to judge Israel. We will take more of a look at Gideon in this week's day 4 exercise, but for now, this passage clearly indicates a second function of the judges.

Judges 6:33–35; 7:1–3

33 Now all the Midianites, Amalekites and other eastern peoples joined forces and crossed over the Jordan and camped in the Valley of Jezreel. 34 Then the Spirit of the LORD came on Gideon, and he blew a trumpet, summoning the Abiezrites to follow him. 35 He sent messengers throughout Manasseh, calling them to arms, and also into Asher, Zebulun and Naphtali, so that they too went up to meet them.

⁷:¹ Early in the morning, Jerub-Baal (that is, Gideon) and all his men camped at the spring of Harod. The camp of Midian was north of them in the valley near the hill of Moreh. ² The LORD said to Gideon, "You have too many men. I cannot deliver Midian into their hands, or Israel would boast against me, 'My own strength has saved me.' ³ Now announce to the army, 'Anyone who trembles with fear may turn back and leave Mount Gilead.'" So twenty-two thousand men left, while ten thousand remained.

- Who are Gideon's men and where do they come from (6:34–35; 7:1)? What does he call them to? What does Yahweh call Gideon's men (7:3)?

- What function/role does the judge play in these verses?

Finally, four verses found in the book of Judges provide additional insight into the role of the judges.

Judges 3:11

So the land had peace for forty years, until Othniel son of Kenaz died.

Judges 3:30 (Ehud)

That day Moab was made subject to Israel, and the land had peace for eighty years.

Judges 5:31 (Deborah)

"So may all your enemies perish, LORD!
    But may all who love you be like the sun
    when it rises in its strength."

Then the land had peace forty years.

Judges 8:28

Thus Midian was subdued before the Israelites and did not raise its head again. During Gideon's lifetime, the land had peace forty years.

- Highlight the repeated phrase that appears in each verse.
- Look up these verses in at least three other translations. Write down how these other translations render this phrase.

What these verses indicate is that the term *judge* "signifies the action that restores [*shalom*] to a community after it has been disturbed."[5] In other words, the judge had a responsibility to "restore the community's equilibrium."[6]

Real People, Real Places, Real Faith

As we've discussed, during the days of the judges, Israel was still a decentralized tribal confederation. This means Israel had no central government (a.k.a. no monarchy). Why is that important? No central government means no taxes. No taxes means no federal funding. No federal funding means no federally sponsored projects like roads, palaces, temples, or fortifications. It also means *no professional army*. The only way for Israel to fight its battles was for someone to go to the clans and convince them to volunteer their men of fighting age to march out to war. Saying yes to this call to muster meant that houses and fences would go unbuilt; harvests would be left in the fields; women, children, and resources left undefended; and all the domestic tasks of milking, pruning, fleecing would be left in the hands of women, children, and the elderly. It also meant the loss of life of the most physically competent citizens of Israel's young nation. In other words, saying yes was costly. And where does a volunteer army get its weapons? You've likely heard the phrase "They will beat their swords into plowshares and their spears into pruning hooks" (Isa 2:4). Well, the process could go the other way as well—regular citizens

---

5 Koehler and Baumgartner, *Hebrew and Aramaic Lexicon*, 2:1623.
6 Stone, *Judges*, 188.

transforming their farming tools into the weapons of warfare. In sum, in this decentralized, tribal society—where each individual's loyalty was directed first to their clan and then to their tribe—the defense of the nation was both voluntary and nonprofessional. It was the judge's task to unify this association of neighboring states to defend the common good. And if he or she couldn't rally the troops, successfully reining in the rowdy residents of Israel's "Wild West," and if he or she did not carry the sort of gravitas that would motivate a nation of "smallholder" farmers to fight for their future, then the kingdom would fail.

Our People, Our Places, Our Faith

As we conclude this lesson, let's reflect on some of the things we've learned about our protagonist.

Make a list of what you learned about Deborah (think about her place in her society, the opportunities typically afforded to women in her world, the norms her calling seemed to violate, how she responded to her calling, how others responded to her):

In what ways do you relate to her? Personally, vocationally, professionally?

If you found yourself in a similar spot, what do you think your response would have been?

In what ways can you mimic Deborah and embrace your calling with the sort of self-confidence and gravitas that stirred the tribes to action?

Day 2: A Prophet

First Contact

If I were to ask you who is the servant of the Secret Fire; wielder of the Flame of Anor; bearer of Narya, the ring of fire; could you answer? And if so, would you name him Mithrandir, Tharkûn, or Olórin? Or might you know him best as *Gandalf*? And would your heart leap like mine at the mention of his name? What is it about characters like Gandalf that inspire us to be better than we are? Is it that they can see the face of a king under a Ranger's hood? Is it that the power they carry within allows them to stand alone against the Balrog on the bridge? Is it that even in our darkest hour, when Gandalf says we're safe, we believe him?

Into the Book

The prophet of Israel is where the Gandalfs and Dumbledores of fantasy fiction meet their archetype. Like Gandalf, the prophet is known by many names: "man of God," "seer," "dreamer of dreams," "servant of the Most High," and most arresting to me, "the mouth of Yahweh." But if you truly know the prophet of Israel, you know him or her as the "one summoned" to first hear and then deliver the word of God, the Hebrew term is *nabi*. This is the technical term utilized in the book of Deuteronomy to identify the theocratic office of "prophet." They're not just a person who periodically offers a word of prophecy, or engages in some sort of ecstatic utterance, or even sees a vision or predicts the future. No, the *nabi* is one of the three human officers Yahweh entrusted with his kingdom: prophet, priest, and king.

You might be thinking, "A prophet? Why are we talking about prophets?" Take a look at Judges 4:4: "Now Deborah, **a prophet**, the wife of Lappidoth, was leading Israel at that time." That's right. Not only was Deborah Israel's only recorded female judge, she was also a prophet. So let's review the office of the prophet.

Read the following passages and answer the questions.

Deuteronomy 18:15–18

¹⁵ The LORD your God will raise up for you a prophet like me [Moses] from among you, from your fellow Israelites. You must listen to him. ¹⁶ For this is what you asked of the LORD your God at Horeb on the day of the assembly when you said, "Let us not hear the voice of the LORD our God nor see this great fire anymore, or we will die."

¹⁷ The LORD said to me: "What they say is good. ¹⁸ I will raise up for them a prophet like you from among their fellow Israelites, and I will put my words in his mouth. He will tell them everything I command him."

• Who raises up the prophet?

• Who does the prophet represent?

• What words are the prophet supposed to speak?

• What responsibility do the people have regarding the prophet (v. 15)?

Jeremiah 1:4–7

⁴ The word of the LORD came to me, saying,

⁵ "Before I formed you in the womb I knew you,
    before you were born I set you apart;
  I appointed you as a prophet to the nations."
⁶ "Alas, Sovereign LORD," I said, "I do not know how to speak; I am too young."
⁷ But the LORD said to me, "Do not say, 'I am too young.' You must go to everyone I send you to and say whatever I command you."

- Four times in verse 5 the Lord begins a sentence with "I [verb] you." Circle those four things.

- From verse 5, write down what you know about the way one becomes a prophet—is the office inherited or is the prophet chosen?

- Jeremiah's response in verse 6 is telling. Circle what Jeremiah says he does not know how to do. Nowhere prior to Jeremiah's response do we find that the Lord instructed him to speak. What does this imply that Jeremiah knew about prophets?

- The Lord tells Jeremiah in verse 7 exactly what he must do. Highlight those two things.

Let's look at one more function of the prophet. This time we will look at Samuel, the last judge of Israel, who was also a priest and a prophet.

1 Samuel 10:1, 24

^{10:1} Then Samuel took a flask of olive oil and poured it on Saul's head and kissed him, saying, "Has not the LORD anointed you ruler over his inheritance?"

²⁴ . . . Then the people shouted, "Long live the king!"

1 Samuel 16:13

¹³ So Samuel took the horn of oil and anointed him [David] in the presence of his brothers, and from that day on the Spirit of the LORD came powerfully upon David.

- What does Samuel's act of pouring oil and anointing signify in these verses? In other words, for what position did the prophet anoint Saul and David?

1 Samuel 13:13–14; 15:26

[13:13] "You [Saul] have done a foolish thing," Samuel said. "You have not kept the command the Lord your God gave you; if you had, he would have established your kingdom over Israel for all time. [14] But now your kingdom will not endure; the Lord has sought out a man after his own heart and appointed him ruler of his people, because you have not kept the Lord's command."

[15:26] But Samuel said to him, "I will not go back with you. You have rejected the word of the Lord, and the Lord has rejected you as king over Israel!"

- What message from the Lord did the prophet deliver to the king?

Real People, Real Places, Real Faith

The prophets in Israel were public figures. They had access to kings, and when they addressed the nation, you can be sure they drew a crowd! In the days of the judges, prior to the monarchy, the judges were responsible to lead the people militarily and spiritually. Their job was not easy, but it was straightforward: *model* to the citizenry what it looks like to keep the covenant and *confront* the people when they fail. (When the monarchy matures, this will be the king's job.) But what happens when the leaders become corrupt? When the judges and kings are the ones leading the people into rebellion against the covenant? That was when the prophet stepped in as God's spokesperson, defender of the covenant, the "one summoned" to first *hear* the word of Yahweh and then to announce it to his wayward people. Now ponder Deborah for a moment. She was both a judge (Yahweh's *representative* to the people) and a prophet (Yahweh's *spokesperson* to the people). From the perspective of her people, Deborah was a double threat. From the perspective of her God, Deborah was twice to be trusted. She was the system. And she was the checks and balances *to* the system. And whereas one might be *born* a priest or a king, and therefore be vulnerable to the sort of compromise that nepotism and trust funds can create, neither the office of the judge nor the office of the prophet was inherited. Yahweh supernaturally chose these individuals and then confirmed his choice with the empowering of his Spirit. Impressed yet?

Our People, Our Places, Our Faith

In what ways do you sometimes find yourself looking at the things you know need to get done to expand the influence of the kingdom in your family, your church, or your community and feel powerless to do anything about them?

What do you feel like you would need in order to actually change any of those things? (More education? More money? More influence?)

If you had a coffee date with Deborah this Thursday, what do you think she might have to say about all that? By the way, she likes medium roast ... and she takes her coffee black.

Day 3: An Arbitrator (and Her Tree)

First Contact

During the summer of 2005, Kathy spent three weeks in Costa Rica in a Spanish language immersion program. Although she had traveled extensively in Spanish-speaking spaces, she was still struggling with fluency. Hence the time in Costa Rica! What did she learn? More Spanish for sure. But she also learned that in Costa Rica there were no street addresses. Not for houses, businesses, schools, churches, *nada*. Instead they have *direcciones*. English translation? "Directions." So in lieu of street addresses you get landmarks—"Two blocks from the football stadium" or "three houses north of the school" or, my favorite, "close to the old fig tree." Oh my!

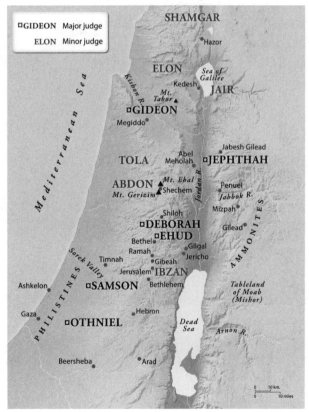

Map of Israel's Judges

Into the Book

One more thing we need to know about Deborah is found in **Judges 4:5**.

[5] She held court under the Palm of Deborah between Ramah and Bethel in the hill country of Ephraim, and the Israelites went up to her to have their disputes decided.

- In the verse provided, circle the location names. Now look at your map; find these places and circle them on the map.
- Underline what Deborah did "under the Palm of Deborah."
- Underline the reason why the Israelites "went up to her."

Now read the following verses from **Exodus 18:13–16**.

[13] The next day Moses took his seat to serve as judge for the people, and they stood around him from morning till evening. [14] When his father-in-law saw all that Moses was doing for the people, he said, "What is this you are doing for the people? Why do you alone sit as judge, while all these people stand around you from morning till evening?"

[15] Moses answered him, "Because the people come to me to seek God's will. [16] Whenever they have a dispute, it is brought to me, and I decide between the parties and inform them of God's decrees and instructions."

- Underline what Moses did in verse 13. Also circle the word used to define Moses's role.
- Underline the reasons why the people come to Moses (vv. 15–16).
- Looking at your underlining in the verses, compare Deborah's job description with Moses's job description. What does this tell you about Deborah's role and standing in the community?

You might be wondering about the "Palm of Deborah" and asking what the tree has to do with anything. As you just observed, the tree served as the location of Deborah's court. And just as the people knew where to find Moses to take their disputes to him, the Israelites knew where to find Deborah to take their disputes to her. Let's look at a couple more references to trees as landmarks in the Bible.

Read the following passages. In each passage,

- highlight the name of the tree,
- and, using a different color, highlight the names of the people (including the Lord) involved.

Judges 4:5–7; 6:11–12

[4:5] [Deborah] held court under the Palm of Deborah between Ramah and Bethel in the hill country of Ephraim, and the Israelites went up to her to have their disputes decided. [6] She sent for Barak son of Abinoam from Kedesh in Naphtali and said to him, "The Lord, the God of Israel, commands you: 'Go, take with you ten thousand men of Naphtali and Zebulun and lead them up to Mount Tabor. [7] I will lead Sisera, the commander of Jabin's army, with his chariots and his troops to the Kishon River and give him into your hands.'"

[6:11] The angel of the Lord came and sat down under the oak in Ophrah that belonged to Joash the Abiezrite, where his son Gideon was threshing wheat in a winepress to keep it from the Midianites. [12] When the angel of the Lord appeared to Gideon, he said, "The Lord is with you, mighty warrior."

Genesis 12:6–7; 18:1–2, 10

[12:6] Abram traveled through the land as far as the site of the great tree of Moreh at Shechem. At that time the Canaanites were in the land. [7] The Lord appeared to Abram and said, "To your offspring I will give this land." So he built an altar there to the Lord, who had appeared to him.

[18:1] The Lord appeared to Abraham near the great trees of Mamre while he was sitting at the entrance to his tent in the heat of the day. [2] Abraham looked up and saw three men standing nearby. When he saw them, he hurried from the entrance of his tent to meet them and bowed low to the ground.

[18:10] Then one of them said, "I will surely return to you about this time next year, and Sarah your wife will have a son."

- Whose words do the messengers speak in all four of these passages?

- Have you noticed that in each of the passages, trees mark places where divine messages are delivered?

Real People, Real Places, Real Faith

When I first started visiting Israel, I found the climate and topography quite exotic. I'd never lived anywhere where the sun shone every day, it rained only three months out of the year, and little (mostly bald) mountains popped up out of seemingly nowhere. I'd never been anywhere where you could be slogging through snow on the streets of Jerusalem and then, a mere forty-five-minute drive later, find yourself hiking in shorts and a T-shirt in Jericho. The dry gulleys (known to the locals as *wadis*) that turned into raging rivers during the wet season, the citrus groves in every open agricultural space, and temperatures that reached 100 degrees by midday but dropped to 65 at night were all new to me. And no humidity! Craziness. I became accustomed to hanging out my dig clothes at 2:00 p.m. only to collect them fully dry by 2:35 p.m. I learned to recognize the particular smell of the limestone soil—and to keep an eye out for enormous beetles and scorpions on dig sites! And waking up every morning to the cooing of the doves? Priceless. Then I moved to Southern California. And I found out Israel wasn't exotic at all! It was simply a "Mediterranean climate." And because it was a Mediterranean climate, trees (such as Deborah's palm tree) were super important and not nearly as common there as they are in the humid continental climate of my native northeastern United States.

Our People, Our Places, Our Faith

As we engage the epic tale of Deborah and Barak, we need to regularly remind ourselves that we are talking about *real* people who lived in *real* places and that their daily lives were shaped by their real space just as much as ours are. So just as I—an East Coast girl for whom the mountains are tall, the pines are thick, creeks are common, and rain and snow are weekly events—found the land of Israel unique and exotic, you might find Deborah's Israel unique and exotic too. Which means we have to work extra hard to put aside *our* world and imagine *their* world as it actually was. In my world in Massachusetts, naming a single tree as a landmark would be laughable. Trees are everywhere! But in Deborah's world, a three-hundred-year-old oak, an olive tree twice or three times that age, or a towering Judean date palm would indeed draw attention, become a landmark, and as you've seen, be utilized by the locals for *direcciones*![1]

---

1   Oded Borowski, *Agriculture in Iron Age Israel* (Boston: American Schools of Oriental Research, 2002), 23–26.

Day 4: Meet the Judges

Gideon

5

Gideon

Meaning of name: "Hacking man" or "cutting man"

Family background: Son of Joash the Abiezrite

Title given: Mighty warrior

Israel's disobedience: Did not listen to Yahweh; worshiped the gods of the Amorites; served Baal and Asherah

Empowerment: Given the word of the Lord and the promise that he would be with Gideon; the Spirit of the Lord came on him

Oppressor: Midianites

Length of oppression: Seven years

Length of peace: Forty years

Other information: A.k.a. Jerub-Baal

First Contact

Do you come from a tradition that sometimes speaks of "putting out a fleece"? You might hear an old-timer talking about a big decision in their lives, so they "put out a fleece"—"God, if my mentor from my first job calls me tomorrow morning, I'll take that as a sign that you want me to have that job." The idea is to discern God's will by asking him to provide a tangible, observable sign. In this study, you'll meet the guy who gave us that tradition!

His name is Gideon. His story encompasses three chapters in the book of Judges (6–8) and includes one chapter about his son Abimelek (9). You're not expected to review all of his story now, but when you get a chance, give it a read! The biblical account provides a lot of information about Gideon, including his conversations with "the angel of the LORD" and with "the LORD."

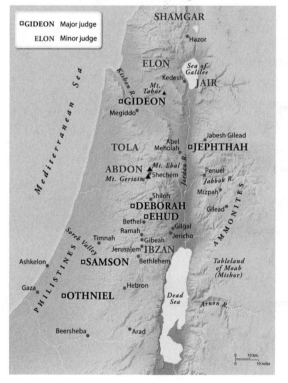

Map of Israel's Judges

Gideon was the son of Joash the Abiezrite, from the tribe of Manasseh. According to Stone, the name Gideon comes from the root meaning "to hack" or "to cut." When the ending -*on* appears on a name, it "generally means that person so named is characterized by the word to which it is attached. So Gideon's name would mean 'hacking man' or 'cutting man.'"[1]

Reading & Observing

- Find **Gideon** on the map and circle his name there.
- Turn in your Bible and read the following Gideon references, noticing his story in the cycle of the judges.

---

1   Stone, *Judges*, 274–75.

Cycle found in Judges 2:11–19	Gideon (Judges 6–8)
Israelites did evil in the eyes of the Lord	6:1
They served other gods, forsook the Lord	6:10
They aroused the Lord's anger	
The Lord gave them/sold them into the hands of raiders/enemies	6:1
The people groaned under the oppression; cried out to the Lord	6:6
The Lord raised up judges who saved them	see 6:8–12, 14
When the judge died, the people returned to following other gods	8:33
Oppressor	6:1–6
Length of peace	8:28
Death notice	8:28, 32, 33

Now read **Judges 6:1–10** and answer the following questions.

• In what specific ways were the Israelites being oppressed? What prompted them to cry out to the Lord?

• Who did Yahweh send when the Israelites cried out and, in your own words, what was his message (vv. 7–10)?

Verses 11–24 recount the conversation between the Lord and Gideon. The Lord calls Gideon to save the Israelites, Gideon is skeptical and asks for a sign, the Lord does as he asks, and Gideon agrees.

Look at **verses 14–16**.

• What does Yahweh tell Gideon to do?

• How does Gideon respond to the Lord? What reason does he give for not being qualified?

• How many times does Yahweh tell Gideon he is sending him or that he will be with him (vv. 11–16)?

Read **6:25–35** and answer these questions.

• What did Gideon tear down and cut down (remember the meaning of his name)? Who were the Israelites worshiping?

• The Lord again empowers Gideon to fight against who (v. 33)?

• What tribes does he call on to help (v. 35)?

Again, Gideon asks for a sign. God gives the sign. Gideon had gathered thirty-two thousand men, which the Lord narrowed down to three hundred so that Israel could not boast (6:36–7:8).

• What is unique about Gideon's death notice (8:28, 32–33)?

• How would you categorize Gideon?

What about those signs? Why did Gideon ask for a sign? Look back at 6:15 where Gideon asks, "How can I save Israel? My clan is the weakest in Manasseh, and I am the least in my family." What does he mean by that? Remember that we are dealing with a tribal society, where seniority ruled and the firstborn male son held a privileged position. In combat, "the eldest son of the ruling clan in the dominant tribe would possess intrinsic authority to lead."[2] How would the tribes perceive Gideon if he were to step outside the societal norms and claim a role of leadership in his clan? And claim leadership *for* his clan? Why did Gideon ask for a sign? He wanted "extraordinary authentication to mark him as God's choice to lead his people."[3]

Responding: What's Your Territory?

In this week's individual lesson, we explored the functions of the judges and the role of the prophet and their responsibilities. The judge was an arbitrator, a military leader, and a spiritual leader. You've seen through some of the judges' studies that Yahweh "raised up" and empowered leaders. And here with Gideon, Yahweh promises that he will be with him. How has he empowered you for the task he has placed before you? I'll ask again:

---

2   Stone, *Judges*, 275.
3   Stone, *Judges*, 275.

- What territory can you see from where you're standing that belongs to the kingdom of God and, for whatever reason, is not yet in the hands of God's people?

- Is it worth fighting for?

- What are you going to do about it?

SESSION 4

Meet Deborah!

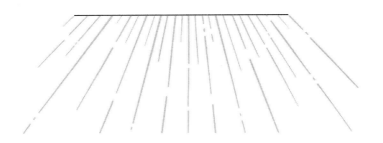

SESSION 4: GROUP MEETING

Schedule

GROUP MEETING
Session 4 Video Teaching and Discussion

INDIVIDUAL STUDY
Day 1: The Players

Day 2: The Playing Field

Day 3: The Assets

Day 4: Meet the Judges—Shamgar

Getting Started

Leader, open your group by first asking if there are any questions regarding the homework and then ask these icebreaker questions.

- When you picture Deborah "the judge," what do you see?
- When you picture Deborah "the prophet," what do you see?
- When you picture Deborah "the commander in chief," what do you see?

Watch Session 4 Video: Meet Deborah! [29 Minutes]

Streaming video access instructions are on the inside front cover of each study guide.

Video Outline

Follow along during the video, take notes, or write down questions and aha moments as you like.

I. Meet Deborah!

    A. Her name, "to lead"

    B. Her husband, a military man

II. Cycle in the book of Judges

    A. Israelites sin, God sends an oppressor

B. Israelites cry out, God sends a judge

III. Functions of the judges

A. Judicial function: the higher court

B. Military function: musters troops for war

C. Legitimacy? Impossible physical acts of prowess!

IV. Deborah's achievements: nothing unique

A. Musters the troops

B. Leads the people against the enemy

C. Wins and secures territory

D. Rules for forty years

V. Deborah's image and attributes

A. Is she a warrior?

1. Considering Antiope, the Amazon general from *Wonder Woman*

2. Considering Agojie, the women's fighting unit from *The Woman King*

B. Socially appropriate role for women was the head of the household: wife, mother, mother-in-law, grandmother, counselor, educator

C. Attributes: courage, self-sacrifice, integrity, and self-discipline to step up and do the hard thing

D. Deborah's appearance never described

VI. Israel's government

A. Israel's theocracy: *theos* (God) + *krateō* (to rule) = ruled by God

B. Yahweh was Israel's king

C. Theocratic offices

1. King/judge: type-man of the nation

2. Priest: a mediator who spoke for the people to God

3. Prophet: a messenger who spoke for God to the people

4. The first two offices (king and priest) are hereditary, but you can't be born a prophet or a judge, you must be *chosen*

VII. Deborah's functions

A. Judge

B. Prophet

C. Arbitrator (The Palm of Deborah)

1. Tree is *named* for her

2. Trees in Israel are used as landmarks and place names

D. An unlikely leader

1. Empowered by the Holy Spirit to lead

2. She was called, and she said yes

Dialogue, Digest & Do

Discuss the following as a group.

- Now that you've met her, how would you describe Deborah?

- Had you ever tried to picture the court system of Israel before? Select a volunteer to read **Deuteronomy 17:8–13** aloud. What sounds familiar and what's not so familiar?

- What do you make of judges as military commanders and the fact that Deborah wasn't actually on the field of battle? Do you think the biblical narrator is disqualifying her as a "judge" because she isn't engaged in hand-to-hand combat?

- Remembering Deborah as a member of a patriarchal society, where a woman's place was in the domestic sphere, discuss the fact that she is serving as commander in chief of Israel's *army*. Discuss what her unique role communicates about her character and abilities.

- Most of Deborah's peers would be homemakers, competing over the status of their husbands and children. If you were Deborah, how would you feel about being elevated to the role of judge? What might you be thinking and feeling about this distinctive role?

- In your homework you also met Gideon, the judge after Deborah. How does Gideon's response to his crisis and his calling compare with Deborah's?

- Who in your group has never considered themselves a leader? Why? Why might Deborah have said *she* was not a leader?

Next Week

Before next week's group meeting, work your way through the four days of the session 4 individual study. In the study this week, you'll meet a few good guys and bad guys and gain some insight into the crisis facing Deborah and the Israelites.

Closing Prayer

Leader, ask your group members if there is anything they would like prayer for, especially something highlighted by this week's video.

Israel's Promised Tribal Allotments

SESSION 4: INDIVIDUAL STUDY

Deborah's Crisis
in the Valley

The lessons found in the individual studies focus on the *upcoming* week's video lecture.

A Word from Sandy

In our study of Gideon last week, I was struck by Gideon's response when God called him to serve. The text reports that the angel of the Lord appeared to Gideon and said to him, "[Yahweh] is with you, mighty warrior" (Judg 6:12)! Not a bad start! I know that if I were out doing my yardwork and an angel showed up and named me a "mighty warrior," I'd find that super affirming and motivating. But did you notice Gideon's response? "Pardon me, my lord, . . . but if [Yahweh] is with us, why has all this happened to us? Where are all his wonders that our ancestors told us about when they said, 'Did not the LORD bring us up out of Egypt?' But now [Yahweh] has abandoned us and given us into the hand of Midian" (v. 13).

Before our study is done, I'm going to talk about "stories that matter" and will argue that Deborah's is one of them. If the phrase "stories that matter" has you thinking about Samwise Gamgee's impassioned speech to a certain despairing ring bearer on the slopes of Mount Doom, you're right on target. The great narratives of the Old Testament have been preserved for us for a *reason*. Rehearsing these stories to each other reminds us of who we are. It reminds us of who our God is. "Stories that matter" *strengthen* us. When I am facing a great challenge, an impossible battle, a diagnosis that has brought me to my knees, a truly hopeless scenario—just like Gideon—the only thing that gets me back on my feet is reminding myself who I serve. If the God I serve is the God of the exodus, the conquest, and the resurrection, then there is real hope, real strength, a real reason to get back in the game.

But what if I don't know the God of the exodus, the conquest, and the resurrection? What if the God I've come to know is the God of shallow pop songs and "feel good" motivational speeches? What if I've never stood on the edge of the Jezreel Valley with Deborah and Barak, looked into the face of the impossible, and chosen to act all the same? Then I'm in trouble. And so is the kingdom.

Day 1: The Players

Real Time & Space

As you read about in session 1, during the Late Bronze Age (1550–1200 BCE), Canaan was occupied by the Egyptian Empire. As a result, the political and economic infrastructure of Canaan became extremely dependent on Egypt. In his classic textbook *Archaeology of the Land of the Bible*, Israeli archaeologist Amihai Mazar names this chapter of Canaan's story "In the Shadow of Egyptian Domination." The Jezreel Valley and the city of Megiddo were specific targets of Egyptian control. The Jezreel Valley was a target because of its rich agricultural land. The Egyptians established their own royal estates in the valley, and records demonstrate that they had controlled the produce from those plantations for centuries. In fact, the Amarna letters (fourteenth-century-BCE correspondence between the pharaohs and the Canaanite rulers) record Egypt's expectation that these Canaanite kinglets would provide the forced labor necessary to cultivate these plantations. Megiddo was a target because it was one of only three points of entry into the valley. Regarding this massive and massively important urban center, Pharaoh Thutmose III is famous for saying, "To capture Megiddo, is to capture a thousand cities!" Indeed, if you controlled Megiddo, you controlled the Jezreel Valley, the Via Maris that ran through it, and all the trade and military activity that touched northern Canaan. Not a bad deal.

As the Late Bronze Age drew to a close, however, Egypt started having trouble at home. So they withdrew into their own boundaries, and all the wealth of Canaan was up for grabs. This is where our villains Jabin and Sisera enter the picture. Apparently these two have teamed up to control the region for themselves. In Judges 4:2 we see that Sisera, the commander of Jabin's army, was based in Harosheth Haggoyim, a place name that means "the places plowed by the nations." These are most likely those long-standing Egyptian royal estates located east of Megiddo. Take another look at Judges 4:1–3. Here our heroes are being "cruelly oppressed." Likely our team is being forced into the role of plantation slaves in Harosheth Haggoyim, but this time by Jabin and Sisera!

First Contact

Every great story needs a great plotline. According to the experts, great plotlines are created by conflict. Who would have thought? And where does conflict come from? The good guys against the bad guys, of course! And so we launch: exposition, rising action, climax! Next, cue the falling action and resolution. Who resolves conflict? Heroes. And the more complicated our hero, the better. Man versus man. Man versus self. Man versus nature. Strap into your seats, ladies and gentlemen, this story has it all!

Into the Book

Map of Israel's Judges

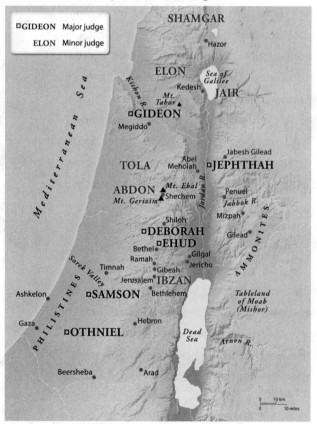

- Locate and circle **Hazor** (in the far north).
- Find **Deborah** on the map and circle her name.
- Looking to the north again, find and circle **Kedesh** in the tribal territory of Naphtali. (This is southwest of the Sea of Galilee.)

For your introduction to some of the cast of characters of good guys and bad guys, read **Judges 4:1–6a** and answer the questions after.

¹ Again the Israelites did evil in the eyes of the LORD, now that Ehud was dead.
² So the LORD sold them into the hands of Jabin king of Canaan, who reigned in Hazor. Sisera, the commander of his army, was based in Harosheth Haggoyim.
³ Because he had nine hundred chariots fitted with iron and had cruelly oppressed the Israelites for twenty years, they cried to the LORD for help.

⁴ Now Deborah, a prophet, the wife of Lappidoth, was leading Israel at that time. ⁵ She held court under the Palm of Deborah between Ramah and Bethel in the hill country of Ephraim, and the Israelites went up to her to have their disputes decided. ⁶ She sent for Barak son of Abinoam from Kedesh in Naphtali.

- Highlight the names and titles of the "bad guys" and their locations in verse 2.
- Using a different color, highlight the names of the "good guys" and their locations in verses 4 and 6.
- What reasons does the narrator give for the Israelites crying out to the Lord?

Real People, Real Places, Real Faith

We have learned that in the days of Deborah the Israelites are **enslaved** as forced laborers on the plantations of Harosheth Haggoyim. We have agonized with them as they have suffered under the **cruel oppression** of foreign rulers and searched the horizon for a deliverer who could shake off their shackles and give them back a future and a hope.

Have you, perchance, recognized in *this* story the echoes of another story in Scripture?

Exodus 1:11–14 tells us that the Egyptians "put slave masters over [the Israelites] to **oppress** them with forced labor, and they built Pithom and Rameses as store cities for Pharaoh. But the more they were **oppressed**, the more they multiplied and spread; so the Egyptians came to dread the Israelites and worked them **ruthlessly**. They made their lives **bitter** with **harsh labor** in brick and mortar and with all kinds of work in the fields; in all their **harsh labor** the Egyptians worked them **ruthlessly**."

As we approach the story of Deborah and Barak, we need to recognize that this is not a *new* story for the Israelites. They've been here before. And in the archive of their memories, another "story that matters" speaks directly to this moment of crisis—the power of Yahweh's rescue and redemption in the midst of equally cruel oppression. But notice that whereas Exodus speaks of Yahweh having *bought* his people back from Egypt, the story here in the book of Judges states that he "*sold* them into the hands of Jabin" (4:2, emphasis added). Why? Because here in cycle four of the book of Judges, the Israelites have once again done "evil in the eyes of the LORD" (4:1). Our heroes are right back in that awful place. Perhaps it is time for our forefathers in the faith to own their responsibility in this scenario of despair? Perhaps, in the words of Taylor Swift, "Hi, I'm the problem, it's me."[1]

Our People, Our Places, Our Faith

We have talked a lot in this study about unlikely heroes. Situations in which the enemies and opposition to the kingdom *seem* impenetrable, but with the power of the Holy Spirit are anything but.

Name a situation of opposition to kingdom-building you have experienced. Did the Spirit bring victory? How?

What role did you play in this scenario? Were you the one bringing resolution, or were you, perhaps, the one responsible for creating the problem?

Think of a current situation where you believe kingdom-building is being thwarted. In what ways might you lay hold of the power of the Spirit and the character of God to move your community toward victory?

---

[1]   Taylor Swift, "Anti Hero," *Midnights*, Republic Records, 2002.

Day 2: The Playing Field

First Contact

If you've ever played sports or are an avid sports fan, you're familiar with the term home-court or home-field advantage. The idea is that a team playing on their own field has an advantage over the visiting team. The enthusiasm of the home crowd and the additional rest from not having to travel both play a role for sure. But what about the actual arena of the competition? Think about a cross-country race. If you're on your home course, you know every hill, every turn, every obstacle, every water hazard. You know where the footing is solid and where you need to slow your pace, *and* you already have your own mile markers mapped out in your head. You know things the visiting team doesn't know. You have a home-field advantage.

Into the Book

Yesterday we began looking at the good guys and bad guys and where they are located. Today we'll look more closely at the places where the upcoming battle takes place.

The map included here shows the route of the Via Maris (which you heard about in session 1). Recall that this superhighway connects Egypt to Mesopotamia by way of Israel.

Locate **Hazor** on the map.

- What about Hazor's location do you think would make this city desirable?

Via Maris Trade Route

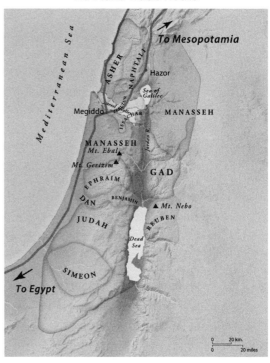

107

• In what Israelite tribal territory is Hazor found?

You've already found Megiddo on the map of the judges from yesterday's work. If you need to take a look to remind yourself, go ahead!

• Megiddo lies on the southern edge of what valley?

• Where does Megiddo fall in relation to the Via Maris? (Feel free to add Megiddo to the map with the Via Maris.)

• What is significant about Megiddo's location on the Via Maris? (You may want to look back at session 1.)

• List here the tribes whose allotments fall in this valley.

• What are some insights you can draw about the geography and the potential strategic placement of the cities named in our narrative? Where might you want to call home and why?

Real People, Real Places, Real Faith

As we've seen, the period of the book of Judges describes an era when everything from small-scale skirmishes to all-out warfare was frequent. We know something about what warfare looks like in our day, but what might it have looked like in theirs?

Offensive weapons can be divided into three categories: **short-range** weapons used in hand-to-hand combat (sword, dagger, shield, spear, and mace); **medium-range** weapons designed to be thrown for a short distance (sometimes a spear; always the javelin); and **long-range weapons** that kept the soldier on the offensive but out of range of his opponent (the sling, and the bow and arrow). One of the most detailed descriptions of weaponry in the Bible is the battle of David and Goliath in 1 Samuel 17. And our narrator revels in offering us every detail of who is equipped with what!

First we hear of Saul's armor. As king, even of a young nation, Saul would've had the good stuff. In 1 Samuel 17:38–39 Saul attempts to dress David in *his* armor: a tunic first, then a coat of armor, a bronze helmet, and a sword. We can't know if Saul's sword was bronze or iron. Iron would of course be best but also way harder to obtain at the beginning of the Iron Age.

David chooses instead his own clothes (no armor), his shepherd's staff (hand-to-hand combat), his sling (medium or long range), and five stones from the wadi. In contrast, Goliath's armor—Goliath being a professional who had "been a warrior from his youth" (v. 33)—is so extensive that the Hebrew narrator doesn't have vocabulary for it all! Goliath wears a bronze helmet, a hefty coat of scale armor (also made of bronze), bronze greaves (shin armor), and a bronze javelin! He had a spear "like a weaver's rod" (meaning the spear had a loop attached so that the warrior could put a spin on it at release, similar to an excellent spin on a passed football), and the spear *had an iron point* (vv. 4–7). Goliath also had his own personal shield bearer (v. 41). I've always wanted one of those.

The point of these descriptions? David is completely outgunned. Hand-to-hand combat? Not a chance. Medium range? He's in trouble. But *long-range* . . . hmm, our young hero might have a chance. When we pause to remember that "slingers" were standard members of ancient armies, that slingstones were often made of basalt, that a slingstone could travel at as much as 150 miles per hour (take *that* Nolan Ryan), well, now we're cooking. And when we further pause to consider that Goliath was a very large man carrying over a hundred pounds of armor and weaponry, and David is a boy carrying only a sling and a pouch, even if our young hero's aim had failed him, he could have outrun Goliath in a heartbeat! Instead, David engages from a distance, brings down the warrior with his slingstone, sprints over to his fallen foe to grab his sword, and uses the giant's own sword to dispatch his opponent. Not a bad plan, David!

Our People, Our Places, Our Faith

In what ways do you, like David and our heroes from the days of the judges, feel like you've been called to a gunfight with nothing but a switchblade and some duct tape? Describe the situation.

Consider the times you have been left with only one weapon to fight with: prayer. Write a bit about how this tool, this weapon, wields the power of God. Does what you've written change your perspective on "showing up to a gunfight with a switchblade"? Dear ones, never underestimate the weapon God has placed in your hands!

Day 3: The Assets

First Contact

Who doesn't love the cult classic *The Princess Bride*? Do you remember the scene where Inigo Montoya and Fezzik carry a "mostly dead" Westley to the castle to stop the wedding of Westley's beloved Buttercup from the evil Prince Humperdinck? After swallowing the "miracle pill," the newly awakened (but still paralyzed) Westley asks Inigo, "What are our liabilities?" Inigo responds, "There is but one working castle gate . . . and it is guarded by sixty men." "And our assets?" Westley queries. "Your brains, Fezzik's strength, and my steel." Westley's response? "Impossible!"

Into the Book

What do we know about Sisera's assets and Israel's assets? Look again at **Judges 4:2–3**.

- List Sisera's assets here.

Next, look at **Judges 5:7–8**.

> ⁷ Villagers in Israel would not fight;
>   they held back until I, Deborah, arose,
>   until I arose, a mother in Israel.
> ⁸ God chose new leaders
>   when war came to the city gates,
> but not a shield or spear was seen
>   among forty thousand in Israel.

• What do these verses indicate about Israel's liabilities? In other words, what *don't* they have?

• What do you count as Israel's assets found in these verses?

Real People, Real Places, Real Faith

As we've discussed, the Israelites did not have a professional army. Neither did they have professional weapons. As a result, we can expect our tribal chieftains to make regular use of what the experts call "irregular warfare"—avoiding large-scale combat and focusing on small, stealthy, hit-and-run engagements. We can also expect a number of our volunteer soldiers to be carrying homemade weapons: clubs (a piece of wood), maces (a stick with a heavy stone or metal attached to the end), axes (either a stone or bronze blade), spears, daggers, and lances. Under the best circumstances, there might be swords.[1] Ehud is a great example here. Likely the closest thing Israel has to a trained assassin, Ehud forges for himself a short double-edged sword, small enough to hide on his thigh (Judg 3:16). That would be his *right* thigh, as our assassin is *left*-handed!

But most of our team would not have been sporting such a professional weapon. The narrator in the book of Judges clues us in to some of Israel's even less conventional weapons. Shamgar kills six hundred Philistines with an "oxgoad" (likely a cattle prod made of wood with a metal tip or spur on the end; 3:31).[2] Gideon goes to battle ("irregular warfare") with *not* the twenty-two thousand who answered the muster but the three hundred street fighters that Yahweh approved. Yahweh defeats the Midianites with trumpets (ram's horns), clay jars, and torches (7:16–25)! Then there was the strongman Samson, who tore a lion apart with his bare hands (14:6), single-handedly defeated thirty men (14:19), set fire to an entire Philistine

---

1   Philip J. King and Lawrence E. Stager, *Life in Biblical Israel* (Louisville: Westminster John Knox, 2001), 224.
2   See Stone, *Judges*, 248 and King and Stager, *Life in Biblical Israel*, 92.

settlement using three hundred foxes-on-fire (15:4), took out a thousand men with a donkey's jawbone (15:15), and killed "many more [Philistines] when he died than while he lived" by pulling down a temple on their heads (16:30)! Unconventional? Perhaps. Effective? You bet!

Our People, Our Places, Our Faith

So how do you respond to all this talk of weapons and warfare in the past. Does it make you uncomfortable? How do you understand it in our new-covenant time today?

Can you recall the "weapons" of Ephesians 6? List them here. Do you have access to those weapons?

As we've learned, the kingdom of God in the new covenant does not expand by means of military acquisition. Rather, as Paul teaches us in the book of Ephesians, "Our struggle is not against flesh and blood, but against the rulers, against the authorities, against the powers of this dark world and against the spiritual forces of evil in the heavenly realms" (6:12).

If the church does not claim new territory by military acquisition, how does the church claim new territory?

So, recognizing that you and your faith community are the current functioning body of God's representatives, write out the ways you can actively respond to the words of Joshua 23:8–9: "You are to hold fast to the Lord your God, as you have until now. The Lord has driven out before you great and powerful nations; to this day no one has been able to withstand you."

Day 4: Meet the Judges

Shamgar

3

Shamgar

Meaning of name: His name is not Hebrew; possibly of Hurrian or Anatolian origin; possibly of the "Sea Peoples" who settled on the coast in the early twelfth century BCE

Family background: Son of Anath

Length as judge: Unknown

Other information: Used an oxgoad to kill six hundred Philistines; he "saved" Israel

---

First Contact

Except for a mention in one verse in **Judges chapter 5**, Shamgar's[1] story begins and ends in **Judges 3:31**.

> 3:31 After Ehud came Shamgar son of Anath, who struck down six hundred Philistines with an oxgoad. He too saved Israel.

> 5:6 "In the days of Shamgar son of Anath,
>> in the days of Jael, the highways were abandoned;
>> travelers took to winding paths.
> 7 Villagers in Israel would not fight;
>> they held back until I, Deborah, arose,
>> until I arose, a mother in Israel."

Map of Israel's Judges

Reading & Observing

- Find **Shamgar** on the map provided (look in the far north) and circle his name.
- Which judge came prior to Shamgar?

- What does Judges 5:6 suggest about the time when Shamgar was active? Who was the other judge leading then?

---

1   See Stone, *Judges*, 247–48 regarding Shamgar's name.

- Compare and contrast Shamgar with Othniel (p. 32), the exemplary judge. List five differences between the two accounts.

- If Othniel is a Captain America–type hero, which superhero would you liken Shamgar to? (There is no right or wrong answer here.)

Responding: What's Your Territory?

Each week, we will revisit these questions. In this week's individual lesson, we explored the players (the good guys and the bad guys) in Deborah's story, talked about the playing field and having the home-field advantage, and finally looked at the assets of both the good guys and the bad guys. As you've learned more this week, think about the assets available to you for whatever Yahweh is asking you to do, and ask yourself these three questions again.

- What territory can you see from where you're standing that belongs to the kingdom of God and, for whatever reason, is not yet in the hands of God's people?

- Is it worth fighting for?

- What are you going to do about it?

SESSION 5

Deborah's Crisis in the Valley

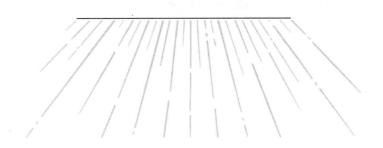

SESSION 5: GROUP STUDY

Schedule

GROUP MEETING
Session 5 Video Teaching and Discussion

INDIVIDUAL STUDY
Day 1: The Plan
Day 2: The Response
Day 3: The Names
Day 4: Meet the Judges—Jephthah

Getting Started

Leader, open your group by asking if anyone has questions about the homework and then ask these icebreaker questions.

- Why is it we all love a good underdog story? Name a favorite and tell the group why you loved it.
- Tell the group a story of the last time you faced a situation where success seemed really hard, maybe even impossible. Did you try anyway? Why?

Watch Session 5 Video:
Deborah's Crisis in the Valley
[25 Minutes]

Streaming video access instructions are on the inside front cover of each study guide.

Video Outline

Follow along during the video, take notes, or write down questions and aha moments as you like.

I. The crisis (Judg 4:1–3)

    A. The fourth cycle

    B. Oppression in the Jezreel Valley—Harosheth Haggoyim

    C. Twenty years!

II. The bad guys

    A. Who are the bad guys?

        1. Jabin the Canaanite, king of Hazor (4:2)

        2. Sisera, commander of Jabin's army, based in Harosheth Haggoyim (Megiddo) (4:2)

    B. Where are the bad guys?

        1. Hazor, astride the Via Maris in the north

        2. Megiddo, controls the entrance to the Jezreel Valley

            a. The capture of Megiddo is the capture of a thousand cities. (Thutmose III of Egypt, 1400s BCE)

    C. What are their assets?

        1. Nine hundred chariots fitted with iron

        2. Eighteen hundred horses

        3. How many troops?

III. The good guys

    A. Who are the good guys?

        1. Deborah (4:4–5): between Ramah and Bethel in the hill country of Ephraim

        2. Barak (4:6): Kedesh in Naphtali

    B. Where are the good guys?

    C. What are their assets?

        1. Ten thousand infantrymen

        2. No chariotry, no iron

        3. Deborah

        4. Yahweh

Dialogue, Digest & Do

Discuss the following as a group.

- Now that you know where Asher, Naphtali, Zebulun, and Issachar are and what gifts the Jezreel Valley has to offer, what are these tribes of Israel losing by "sitting on the sidelines" as Sandy says in the lecture?

- How many of you have seen the movie *The Woman King*? Did you like it? Name one of the powerful moments in that movie and what aspects of the plot/characters/dialogue made it powerful.

- Were you surprised to hear Sandy compare Deborah to Moses? Think again about Deborah's very patriarchal world, yet the narrator announces her words as he does Moses's words. What is the narrator telling you by doing this?

- Discuss the advantage that Sisera's army has in this upcoming battle. What sort of fire-power would his nine hundred chariots, warhorses, and archers have? If you were Sisera and running the battle, what would be your strategy?

- Now talk about Barak and his men. You've done a lot of reading about volunteer armies, "irregular warfare," and homemade weapons. On a level playing field, what sort of chance does Barak have against Sisera? If you were Barak, what might your battle strategy be?

- Under the conditions you've just discussed, are you surprised that *ten thousand* men muster in answer to Barak's call? What does that tell you about Barak? What does that tell you about Deborah? What does that tell you about the ten thousand?

- If you were numbered in that ten thousand, what would you be fighting for? For you, what is worth going to battle for right now?

Next Week

Before next week's group meeting, work your way through the four days of individual study. If you've fallen behind, pick up this week. You'll be doing some more map work, and you'll read an ancient war oracle.

Closing Prayer

Leader, ask your group members if there is anything they would like prayer for, especially something highlighted by this week's video.

Israel's Promised Tribal Allotments

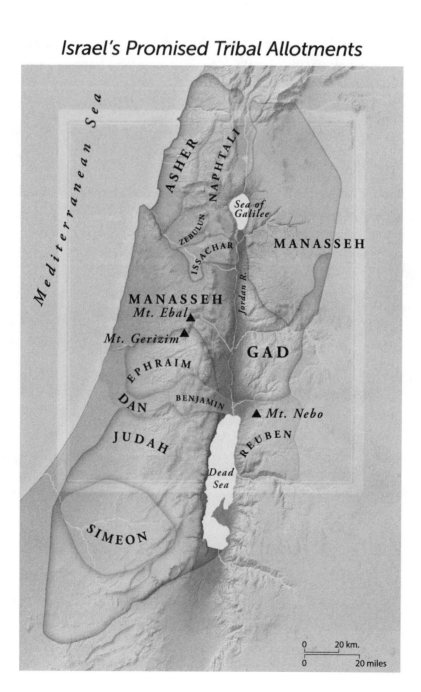

Deborah Musters the Response

The lessons found in the individual studies focus on the *upcoming* week's video lecture.

A Word from Sandy

In our last video session, we were on the edge of our seats as Barak mustered the volunteer troops of Israel to take their stand against Sisera and his chariot forces. For twenty years Israel had been afraid to fight this fight. But under the courageous leadership of Deborah and Barak, the men of Naphtali, Zebulun, Issachar, and Ephraim stepped forward to claim their inheritance. Something had shifted, and Israel was ready to break the cycle.

You also learned a good bit about the "mobile artillery unit" of the ancient world—the chariot! Designed of wood, with a floor of interwoven leather to keep it light, two spoked wheels to make it agile, and an iron axle to make it strong, a chariot was a complete game changer on the ancient battlefield. It was the domestication of the horse, the creation of spoked wheels, and the innovation of bridle and reins that made this new fighting force possible; and it was the wealth of an empire that made them real. Thus, by the days of the exodus (the Late Bronze Age), the chariot dominated international warfare on the coastal plain and valleys of Canaan. The great advantage of the chariot as a war machine was its speed and agility. These assets permitted the chariot to attack the flanks and rear of their opponent's infantry, firing continually while staying out of range of return fire.

When the composite bow was added to the equation, invented around 1700 BCE, that mobile artillery unit could hit a solider as far as 574 feet away, three times the range of a wooden self-bow! Images from New Kingdom Egypt show chariots armed with three or four quivers filled to capacity. Thus, one man drove holding a shield, and a second fired relentlessly. Once the chariot force had succeeded in throwing the enemy's battalions into disarray, then the chariotry would regroup and charge. With their warhorses trained to trample the enemy, on vehicles that could maneuver at twenty-five miles per hour and each chariot containing two men armed to the teeth, how does one go about fighting a chariot force? Well, as military expert S. Weingartner tells us, "It took a chariotry to fight a chariotry." And because the accessories necessary to a chariot unit (the chariot, the horses, coats of mail, composite bow, arrows, etc.) were super expensive, only the superpowers had them. In sum, chariot forces were the nuclear arsenal of Israel's world.

Why am I so interested? Largely because ten thousand men chose to follow Barack to Mount Tabor. Ten thousand men said yes in the context of certain failure. And that stirs something deep inside my heart, something that sounds like courage and feels like hope: "We are hard pressed on every side, but not crushed; perplexed, but not in despair; persecuted, but not abandoned; struck down, but not destroyed" (2 Cor 4:8–9). These men were willing to fight and die for the kingdom because they believed.

Day 1: The Plan

Real Time & Space

Seeking the counsel of the gods before going to war was standard operating procedure in the ancient Near East. Kings would call for one of their many seers or visionaries, whose job it was to speak to the deity on their behalf. The deity's words would then be communicated to the king in the form of a "war oracle"—often some sort of prophetic word regarding the planned battle. In Israel's case, the divine intermediary was the prophet, and the god being consulted, Yahweh. An excellent example of this is found in 1 Kings 22. Here King Jehoshaphat of Judah and King Ahab of Israel are going up against Ramoth Gilead (vv. 2–4). At the prebattle sacrifice, Jehoshaphat asks that they "first seek the counsel of [Yahweh]" (v. 5). But as Ahab has long since stopped listening to Yahweh, he only has prophets of Baal on hand. Jehosphaphat insists, and a prophet of Yahweh is located (v. 8), pulled out of his prison cell, and offers a war oracle to the two allied kings (vv. 17–18). Spoiler alert: Things aren't going to go well for Ahab.

Military leaders would also rely on the *presence* of the prophet in battle. In 1 Samuel 10, Samuel, the prophet, instructs Saul, the new king, to muster the army at Gilgal to engage the Philistines at Mikmash. Saul was to wait seven days for Samuel to come and bless the army and offer the prebattle sacrifice. (By the way, the sacrifice would then become the prebattle barbecue, kind of like carb-loading before a marathon!) Why did Saul want Samuel there? Because the people of Israel were *very* aware that unless God was on their side, they could not win. And as Yahweh's representative, the prophet was the visible manifestation of Yahweh's approval. Have prophet, will travel.

First Contact

Even in ancient times, going to war demanded a detailed military strategy, defined as: "The practice of reducing an adversary's physical capacity and willingness to fight, and continuing to do so until one's aim is achieved."[1] Okay, got it. But how do you do that?

Into the Book

Map of Israel's Judges

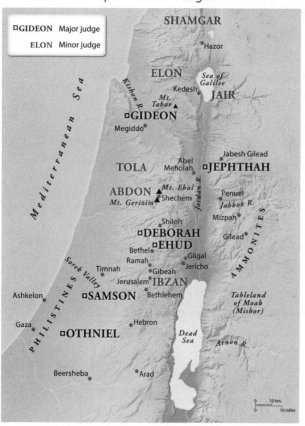

Last week, you circled the locations of the players on this map. Let's do that again here! Circle the names of the good guys and their locations in one color and the locations of the bad guys in a different color. Write in the names of the bad guys by their locations.

- Circle **Deborah**; circle Barak in **Kedesh**.
- Circle **Hazor** (Jabin); circle **Megiddo** and write in "Sisera."

Now read **Judges 4:6–7**.

---

1 Antulio J., Echevarria, II, "What Is Military Strategy?", *Military Strategy: A Very Short Introduction*, Very Short Introductions (New York, 2017; online ed., Oxford Academic, February 23, 2017), https://doi.org/10.1093 /actrade/9780199340132.003.0001.

[6] [Deborah] sent for Barak son of Abinoam from Kedesh in Naphtali and said to him, "The LORD, the God of Israel, commands you: 'Go, take with you ten thousand men of Naphtali and Zebulun and lead them up to Mount Tabor. [7] I will lead Sisera, the commander of Jabin's army, with his chariots and his troops to the Kishon River and give him into your hands.'"

- Deborah calls, and Barak comes. Draw a line on your judges map from **Kedesh** (where Barak was) to Deborah's place between **Bethel** and **Ramah**.
- You also saw this map showing the **Via Maris** last week. To get to Deborah, what road would Barak travel and what valley would he pass through? Who is in that valley?

- Whose words does Deborah speak to Barak? In session 4, we looked at Deborah's roles. In delivering this message, what role is she functioning in?

- On the tribal territory map on the opening page of this session, color in the territories that Yahweh commands Barak to call men from.
- Circle the place on the judges map where Barak is commanded to lead the men to. (Look west of Kedesh.)
- Circle the place where Yahweh will lead Sisera.
- Underline in the verse what Yahweh promises.

Real People, Real Places, Real Faith

How did a prophet deliver a "war oracle" and what does a "war oracle" look like? The idea is that the oracle itself was a direct message from God intended to give guidance to the king. Or in the case of Israel's neighbors, a divine intermediary would inquire of the patron deity of his king (or city) and communicate that message to *his* king. Typically, these messages came via extispicy—the well-worn practice of reading the entrails of slaughtered animals—sometimes through an ecstatic experience. One such example comes from a letter discovered in the royal archives at Mari, an ancient city in Mesopotamia on the Euphrates River.

> In the temple of [Ishtar] in the city, Aḫatum, a servant girl of Dagan-Malik went into a trance and spoke:
>
> "Zimri-Lim: Even though you are neglectful about me, I will massacre on your behalf. Your enemy I will deliver up into your hand. The people that steal from me I will catch, and I will gather them into the camp of Belet-ekallim."[2]

Here a servant girl of Dagon (one of the main gods in Mari) in the temple of Ishtar (the most important female god in Mari) receives a divine message while in a trance, which is then communicated to the king: "Go and fight. I'll be with you and will deliver your enemy 'into your hand' . . . even though you're neglecting me!"

The difference between the oracles spoken by Yahweh and those spoken by any of the other gods? So many things! Let's start with the fact that Yahweh is real. He doesn't need the lungs or livers of sacrificed animals to communicate. He never lies. And when he speaks, the wise king listens!

Our People, Our Places, Our Faith

As we think about territory that we know belongs to the kingdom of God, let's ponder our new-covenant "battle plan." Jesus instructed his disciples, "All authority in heaven and on earth has been given to me. Therefore go and make disciples of all nations, baptizing them in the name of the Father and of the Son and of the Holy Spirit, and teaching them to obey everything I have commanded you. And surely I am with you always, to the very end of the age" (Matt 28:18–20).

What are the original disciples commanded to do?

---

2   Martti Nissinen, *Prophets and Prophecy in the Ancient Near East* (Atlanta: Society of Biblical Literature, 2003), 48.

As this passage continues as the church's "Great Commission," what are we commanded to do?

What is most intimidating about these "marching orders"? List those intimidating issues here—be as personal and as specific as you can.

Now think about what Jesus offers his disciples, and us, to strengthen them in the way. Write it out right here.

You may not be called to leave your country. You may not even be called to leave your neighborhood. But you *are* called. Each of us as a child of God is called to bring the kingdom to our corner of the world, in our own sphere of influence.

So let me ask one more time: Where might your territory be and how are you being called to fight for it?

Day 2: The Response

First Contact

If the first scene of the Civil War movie *Glory* doesn't break you, the last one will. Here, Matthew Broderick, Denzel Washington, and Morgan Freeman depict the courageous efforts of the Fifty-Fourth Massachusetts Volunteer Infantry Regiment—the first Black regiment to fight in the Civil War. The night before the great battle of Fort Wagner, the Black battalion gathers. Morgan Freeman offers a word in the rhythm and rhyme of testimony and prayer: "If tomorrow is our great gettin up mornin', if tomorrow we have to meet the Judgment Day, our heavenly Father, we want you to let our folks know that we died facin' the enemy. We want 'em to know **that we went down standin' up**. . . . We want 'em to know, heavenly Father, that we died for freedom."

Into the Book

Yahweh has laid out his plan and has promised to give Sisera into Barak's hands. How will Barak respond?

Read **Judges 4:8–10**.

⁸ Barak said to [Deborah], "If you go with me, I will go; but if you don't go with me, I won't go."

⁹ "Certainly I will go with you," said Deborah. "But because of the course you are taking, the honor will not be yours, for the LORD will deliver Sisera into the hands of a woman." So Deborah went with Barak to Kedesh. ¹⁰ There Barak summoned Zebulun and Naphtali, and ten thousand men went up under his command. Deborah also went up with him.

- Barak's response in verse 8 is a conditional (if-then) statement. What is your impression of Barak based on this statement? What do you think Barak means by his statement?

- Underline the result of Barak's course.
- Underline what the Lord will do.
- Draw a line on your judges map indicating that Deborah went to Kedesh.

Real People, Real Places, Real Faith

Barak often gets a bad rap because of his words in Judges 4:8, requesting that Deborah go with him. Several modern translations of Deborah's response in verse 9 seem to encourage this bad rap. Take a look at a few. (All emphasis added.)

"Of course I will go with you," Deborah answered. "But *because of your attitude*, you will not be honored when Sisera is defeated." (ERV)

"All right," she replied, "I'll go with you; *but I'm warning you now* that the honor of conquering Sisera will go to a woman instead of to you!" (TLB)

She said, "Of course I'll go with you. *But understand that with an attitude like that*, there'll be no glory in it for you." (MSG)

And she said, "I will surely go with you; nevertheless, the road on which you are going will not lead to your glory, for the LORD will sell Sisera into the hand of a woman." (NRSVue)

Yet the Hebrew is not nearly so condemning, and never once does the narrative indicate that Barak was afraid to fight or hesitant to answer Deborah's call to arms. Rather, a wooden translation of our passage reads more like: "'*Of course I will go with you,*'" she replied. '*But (know that) even (with my presence) your glory will not come from the road upon which you are traveling, rather Yahweh will sell Sisera into the hand of a woman!'"* Indeed, Barak is "all in" from our first introduction to him. In fact, when Deborah summons him (take a look back at your map work yesterday), Barak had to cross enemy lines to answer her summons! There is no indication that he was afraid. Rather, in 5:12 and 5:15 Deborah celebrates Barak's courage. And have we noticed that *ten thousand men* follow Barak into a suicide mission? What kind of man can inspire that sort of loyalty and courage? So, no, Barak is no coward. Rather, Barak's question echoes Moses's and Joshua's battle strategy in Exodus 17:9: "Moses said to Joshua, 'Choose some of our men and go out to fight the Amalekites. Tomorrow I will stand on top of the hill with the staff of God in my hands.'" Why is Moses going to stand on the mountain during the battle? So that the men of arms can see him. And seeing the great prophet of God, they will have confidence that Yahweh is on their side. Apparently, Israel's military knew that "with God we will gain the victory, and he will trample down our enemies" (Ps 60:12). The point here is that Barak wanted God's spokeswoman *with* him. He wanted God's prophet at the battle. Why? (1) She was the only one authorized to speak Yahweh's word when it was "go time!" And (2) her presence would give the men courage.

Our People, Our Places, Our Faith

After his resurrection, Jesus was eating with his disciples and commanded them, "Do not leave Jerusalem, but wait for the gift my Father promised, which you have heard me speak about. For John baptized with water, but in a few days you will be baptized with the Holy Spirit. . . . You will receive power when the Holy Spirit comes on you; and you will be my witnesses in Jerusalem, and in all Judea and Samaria, and to the ends of the earth" (Acts 1:4–5, 8).

In our new-covenant context, Jesus was sending his disciples into a battle. But before sending them to the front lines, what does he send with them? Has this promised changed? Or might it still be yours?

As you go into whatever battle you're facing, whatever territory you have been called to fight for, whose power are you wielding and how will you wield your power?

What are your greatest concerns about "going into battle"?

What are some characteristics of any of the judges you have learned about so far that encourage you? How might you focus on and develop these characteristics in yourself?

Day 3: The Names

First Contact

"What's in a name? That which we call a rose by any other name would smell just as sweet."[1] Recognize the quote? Of course you do. When Juliet (a Capulet) speaks these words to Romeo (a Montague), she is saying that a person's name is not important. As we all know, that doesn't work out too well for these young lovers, because a name *is* important, especially in the ancient Near East.

Into the Book

Throughout the study thus far, we've been looking at the meaning of the names of the judges in the day 4 studies. In your session 4 individual study, you met the players in the Deborah story, the good guys and the bad guys. Today the focus is on the names of those characters and a few others. I've supplied the names (in order of appearance). Fill in the "Title" column and the "Good guy or bad guy?" column for each character in the following table. Turn in your Bible to **Judges 3:15; 4:1–10**.

Real People, Real Places, Real Faith

In the ancient Near East, people often named their children based on the circumstances surrounding their birth. Think of Rachel, Jacob's wife, who with her dying breath named her son Ben-Oni, which means "son of my sorrow" (Gen 35:18). Sometimes parents gave their child a name that was an expression of hope or a symbol for their child. For example, back

---

1 William Shakespeare, *Romeo and Juliet*, ed. W. G. Clark and W. Aldis Wright, Perseus Digital Library, act II, scene ii, lines 43–44, https://www.perseus.tufts.edu/hopper/text?doc=Perseus%3Atext%3A1999.03.0053%3Aact%3D2%3Ascene%3D2.

in session I you saw that Othniel's name means "God (El) is my strength." And Deborah means "may Yahweh lead." Names could be changed, usually by a superior, and often with a change of name came a change of office and therefore destiny. Think for a moment of Abram and Sarai, who became Abraham and Sarah (Gen 17), or Jacob, who became Israel (Gen 32).

Name	Title	Good guy or bad guy?	Meaning of name*
Ehud (3:15; 4:1)			"where is majesty"
Jabin (4:2)			Canaanite name; something like "he will establish understanding" or "may he be wise"†
Sisera (4:2)			Not a Semitic name (not Canaanite, not Hebrew); probably a Philistine name; meaning uncertain
Deborah (4:4)			"Yahweh leads" or "may Yahweh lead"
Lappidoth (4:4)			customary meaning is "torches" but also means "lightning"
Barak (4:6)			"lightning"

* For the information found in this column, see Richard S. Hess, "Israelite Identity and Personal Names from the Book of Judges," *Hebrew Studies* 44 (2003): 25–39; Hess, "The Name Game: Dating the Book of Judges," *Biblical Archeology Review* 30 (2004):38–41; Sasson, *Judges 1–12*; Stone, *Judges*.

†Richter's translation.

Our People, Our Places, Our Faith

When God changed Jacob's name to Israel, Jacob, "he who seizes by the heel" (the second-born trickster who had cheated his brother out of his birthright), was transformed into "he who contends with God." This renaming emerged from the meeting of Jacob and the angel at the Wadi Jabbok and became a major benchmark in Jacob's life. This was the moment when strong and resilient but dishonest Jacob *finally* submitted his intellect, physical strength, and his destiny to the sovereignty of God. And God marked that moment by changing his name.

Do you have a moment like that?

Who were you before?

Who are you now?

Or do you perhaps need to have a moment like that? Write a short prayer asking for the transformation you need.

Day 4: Meet the Judges

Jephthah

8

Jephthah

Meaning of name: Probably short for
Jephthah-El, meaning "God opens [the
womb]"

Family background: Father was Gilead; his
mother a prostitute

Title given: Mighty warrior

Israel's disobedience: Served the Baals,
Astoreths, gods of Aram, gods of Sidon,
gods of Moab, gods of the Ammonites,
and gods of the Philistines

Empowerment: The Spirit of the Lord came
on him

Oppressor: Ammonites and Philistines

Length of oppression: Eighteen years

Length of judgeship: Six years

Other information: Sacrificed his only child

First Contact

Do you remember the story of Jephthah? The story about a warrior who came home from battle and promised that if Yahweh gave him victory, he would sacrifice as a burnt offering whatever came out of his house to meet him? And do you remember who came out? Jephthah's daughter, his only child. Jephthah's story is found in Judges 10–12.

The meaning of his name is probably something like "God opens [the womb]."[1]

Reading & Observing

• Find **Jephthah** on the map and circle his name.

Turn in your Bible to **Judges 10** and read verses **6–16**. Answer the following questions and complete the Jephthah column in the table (use the "Other observations" space to add things that stuck out to you; there are no right or wrong answers).

• How is the oppression the Israelites experienced described in verse 8?

• What strikes you about the Israelites' cry to Yahweh (v. 10)? Compare the cry here with the other accounts of the Israelites' cries. What is different about this one?

3:9

3:15

---

1   Stone, *Judges*, 339.

4:3

6:6

10:10

- Verses 11–16 contain the words of a conversation between Yahweh and the Israelites.
  What does Yahweh say he has done previously?

What does he say he will not do now?

What does he tell them to do?

Map of Israel's Judges

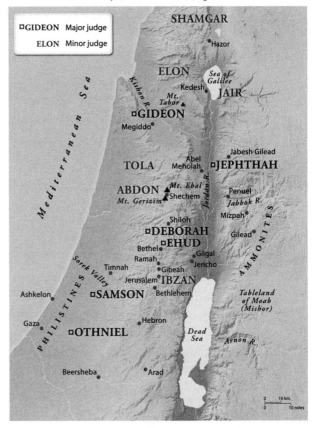

How do the Israelites respond? What kind of repentance do you think this displays?

- In verse 13 Yahweh declares, "I will no longer save you," but in verse 16 he "could bear Israel's misery no longer." What do you think this indicates? Stone describes this as "a shocking collapse of divine resolve," speaking of "divine exasperation, not compassion."[2]

---

2 Stone, *Judges*, 336. See also Isaiah 1:14; 43:24; and Malachi 2:17 for examples of Yahweh's being worn out by Israel's sins.

Responding: What's Your Territory?

Each week, we will revisit these questions. In this week's individual lesson, we looked at the battle plan and Barak's response to the war oracle he received. And we looked into what he meant when he responded that he would go only if the prophet would go with him. Why? Not because he was a coward but because he needed the word of the Lord to lead him. Finally, we looked at names and their importance in the ancient Near East.

Have you been keeping up with journaling your responses each week to these questions? How have your responses developed over our time together so far?

- What territory can you see from where you're standing that you know belongs to the kingdom of God and, for whatever reason, is not yet in the hand of God's people?

- Is it worth fighting for?

- What are you going to do about it?

SESSION 6

Deborah Musters
the Response

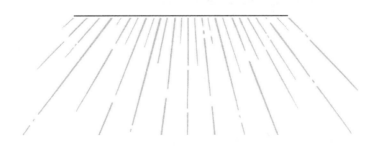

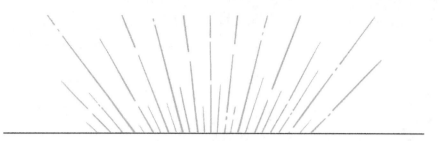

SESSION 6: GROUP MEETING

Schedule

GROUP MEETING

Session 6 Video Teaching and Discussion

INDIVIDUAL STUDY

Day 1: The Traitor

Day 2: The Battle

Day 3: The Victory

Day 4: Meet the Judges—Samson

Getting Started

Leader, open your group by first asking if there are any questions regarding the homework and then ask these icebreaker questions.

- Ask any military families present what it feels like to send a family member off to combat. Tell us a story of a goodbye garbed in camo and the emotions that come with it.
- Has anyone in the group competed in equestrian events? Tell us what it's like to ride a trained and fit horse into a competition.

Watch Session 6 Video: Deborah Musters the Response [28 Minutes]

Streaming video access instructions are on the inside front cover of each study guide.

Video Outline

Follow along during the video, take notes, or write down questions and aha moments as you like.

I. The summons and the muster (Judg 4:6–7)

    A. Deborah summons Barak from Kedesh

        1. The war oracle: the prophet delivers a direct word from his god to the military commander

        2. The plan

            a. Deborah calls (musters) ten thousand men

       b. Go to Mount Tabor

  B. Yahweh summons Sisera to the Kishon River

     1. The strategy in real space

       a. Sisera's location: Megiddo with nine hundred chariots of iron

       b. Barak and his troops' location: Mount Tabor; ten thousand farmers on foot

     2. The military leaders

       a. Sisera: probably a Philistine

       b. Barak: a local; name means "lightning strike"

II. The response (4:8–10)

  A. Barak's response to Deborah: "If you go with me, I will go; but if you don't go with me, I won't go" (4:8).

  B. Septuagint includes: "Because I do not know the day that the LORD will prosper his angel to go with me."

C. Deborah's response to Barak: "Certainly I will go with you. . . . But because of the course you are taking, the honor will not be yours, for the LORD will deliver Sisera into the hands of a woman" (4:9).

Dialogue, Digest & Do

Discuss the following as a group.

- There was some serious action in this session! How did Deborah summoning Barak, giving the war oracle, and then accompanying him to the battlefield strike you? What was expected and what was surprising?

- Describe Barak briefly in terms of modern-day war heroes. Who would you compare him to? Who does he remind you of?

- Sometimes knowing the original languages of the Bible can make a big difference. Sandy talks about how Barak "draws out; musters" his men at Deborah's command because Yahweh is going to "draw out; muster" Sisera. Regardless of what the characters in our story might be thinking, who is really in control of this war?

- What about the Kishon River? Has anyone ever seen a *wadi / barranca* during flood stage? Describe it to the group. If not, from Sandy's description, what do you imagine it to be like?

- When the men of Zebulun and Naphtali gather with Barak on Mount Tabor against the fury of Sisera, what emotions are stirred in your heart as you think of the volunteer troops keeping watch through the night?

- What do you make of the relationship between Deborah and Barak? Is it easy or difficult to imagine today? Why?

Next Week

Before next week's group meeting, work your way through the four days of the individual study. In those individual studies you'll be in the battle with Deborah, Barak, and other players.

Closing Prayer

Leader, ask your group members if there is anything they would like prayer for, especially something highlighted by this week's video.

Israel's Promised Tribal Allotments

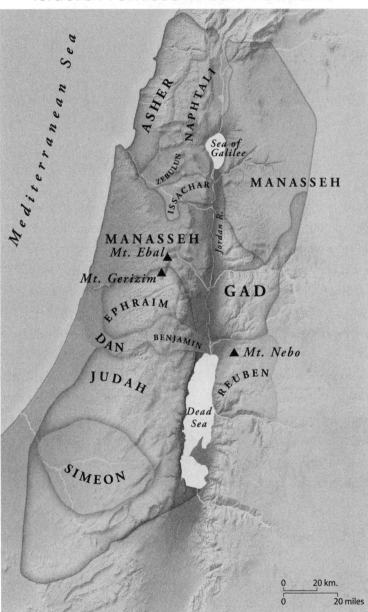

SESSION 6: INDIVIDUAL STUDY

Deborah's Battle and Victory

The lessons found in the individual studies focus on the *upcoming* week's video lecture.

A Word from Sandy

In our last session we met our courageous captain, Barak of Naphtali. We watched as the seasoned judge and prophet Deborah offered him Yahweh's war oracle. "Muster the troops, captain, the hour has come. We're going against Sisera and Jabin!" This was a "mission impossible" if there ever was one. But Barak shows up as the hero we need. His response? "Yes, ma'am, but I'll need you with me." We learned how it was not uncommon for the man of war to keep the prophet close. Saul asked for Samuel. Joshua asked for Moses. Why? Because the prophet spoke for God. And if the military men could see the prophet, they knew that Yahweh couldn't be far behind. Deborah's response? "Yes, I will come with you. But Barak, I should tell you that the honor you are seeking—the death blow to our enemy—will not come at your hand but by the hand of a woman." As with all good war oracles, the thesis statement is a bit vague. First, we the audience are just shocked—a woman? Women don't belong on the battlefield! Then we are confused—which woman? We the audience of course assume he means Deborah. But as with all great storytellers, this narrator is not going to give away the climax of this tale until the very last moment.

Day 1: The Traitor

Real Time & Space

In *The Epic of Eden* I discuss an idea we now know as "fictive kinship." As we've discussed, in Israel's patriarchal culture, an individual's privileges and responsibilities within the *bet ab*, the clan, and the larger society were all predetermined by bloodline, gender, and birth order. The patriarch had the broadest privileges and responsibility, the firstborn son had the next, and all of one's responsibility toward other members of the society was predetermined by blood. The more closely related, the greater the responsibility; the more distantly related, the lesser the responsibility.

So how might a person go about establishing a relationship of privilege and responsibility with someone who was non-kin? Most simply answered, that person would have to *make* kin out of non-kin. This was accomplished by *fictive kinship*. By means of an oath, the people of Israel's world understood that a fictive kinship bond could be established and both parties would thereby agree to *act* like family. Frank Cross puts it this way: "In tribal societies there were legal mechanisms or devices—we might even say legal fictions—by which outsiders, non-kin, might be incorporated into the kinship group."[1] Perhaps the easiest way for us twenty-first-century types to understand this sort of arrangement is to think in terms of marriage and adoption. Even in our present nontribal societies we understand the notion of making nonfamily into family simply by means of a legal agreement. Are the legal responsibilities of an adoptive parent any less than those of a biological parent? Of course not! Through marriage and adoption, two unrelated individuals become family and bear all the responsibilities and privileges that lie therein. This is fictive kinship, and this is the concept that made covenant-making in the ancient Near East ideologically possible. And this is the sort of agreement the tribes of Israel had with the Kenites. And Heber? He was a Kenite.

---

1 Frank Moore Cross, *From Epic to Canon: History and Literature in Ancient Israel* (Baltimore: Johns Hopkins University Press, 1998), 7.

151

First Contact

Benedict Arnold. Judas Iscariot. Brutus. Dr. Smith. What do these folks have in common? They were traitors. They were people of influence who betrayed those who trusted them. And because of their advantaged position as "trusted," they were able to do an incredible amount of damage. Benedict Arnold betrayed his country; Judas Iscariot betrayed his rabbi; Brutus betrayed his friend; Dr. Smith betrayed the entire Lost in Space continuum. Okay, so the last one doesn't have quite the same impact . . .

Into the Book

A new character enters the scene in **Judges 4:11**.

¹¹Now Heber the Kenite had left the other Kenites, the descendants of Hobab, Moses' brother-in-law, and pitched his tent by the great tree in Zaanannim near Kedesh.

- In the verse, circle the name of the new character.
- Underline whom he is a descendant of.
- Underline the place name of where he "pitched his tent," and circle **Kedesh** on the map.

Now look at **Judges 1:16**.

¹⁶ The descendants of Moses' father-in-law, the Kenite, went up from the City of Palms [Jericho] with the people of Judah to live among the inhabitants of the Desert of Judah in the Negev near Arad.

- Moses's father-in-law (Jethro) is originally from which people of Canaan (which of the "-ites")? Underline that in the verse.
- Which tribe had the Kenites become a part of?

- These descendants moved from **Jericho** to **Arad**. Locate and circle these places on the map. (Hints: Jericho is in the Jordan Valley, north of the Dead Sea; Arad is not listed on this map, but it is located eleven miles east of Beersheba in line with the narrow southern portion of the Dead Sea, in the tribal territory of Judah.) Look at the tribal territory map at the opening of this study to refresh your memory of where the tribes are located.

- Now take another look at **4:11**. What is the next thing the narrator tells us after letting us know that Heber is a Kenite?

Map of Israel's Judges

- Draw a line on your map from where the Kenites were living near **Arad** to where Heber moved to. What tribal territory is **Kedesh** located in?

One more piece of valuable information about Heber is this: "There was an alliance between Jabin king of Hazor and the family of Heber the Kenite" (4:17).

- What does this tell you about Heber's loyalty?

153

Real People, Real Places, Real Faith

We've already talked about how names in the ancient Near East were designed to communicate the character and destiny of the name-bearer. What might Heber's name mean? There are several possibilities. In modern Hebrew, Heber could mean "a close friend"; in biblical Hebrew it could be related to the city name "Hebron"; or, most likely, it could refer to a pastoralist group that has not yet settled down.[2] Judges 4 tells us that Heber has made an alliance with Jabin (the bad guy). Perhaps then the meaning of "close friend" communicates "ally" and this is the meaning of Heber's name? But Judges 4 also tells us that Heber is a pastoralist. So perhaps his name is more attached to his profession. Interesting to us is that Heber has chosen to live among Israelites who are all farmers. More interesting is that neither pastoralists nor farmers were "economically self-sufficient"[3]—each depends on trade with the other for survival. So we can anticipate that the Israelites are thinking of Heber as a neighbor, an ally, a trade partner, a kinsman. But Sisera knows Heber to be *his* ally. Thus, the trust that the Israelites have in Heber makes them vulnerable to his betrayal. And because Heber is married, with his own *bêt 'āb*, Heber's entire household must follow him in his alliances. So our girl Jael? As Heber's wife she is by default an ally of Sisera. But there are some courageous folk out there whose allegiance to Yahweh is not for sale. Not for any price.

Our People, Our Places, Our Faith

"It's just business," people say. Or "It wasn't my call." Or there is the perennially juvenile "Well, everyone else was doing it." There are childish representations of this sentiment, and there are adult representations of the same. "Keeping the peace," "choosing my battles," and "maintaining the community" too often become the excuses of cowardice instead of the expressions of measured wisdom they were intended to be.

---

2   Richard S. Hess, "The Name Game," *Biblical Archaeology Review* 30.6 (2004): 38–41, accessed online at https://library.biblicalarchaeology.org/article/the-name-game/; Sasson, *Judges*, 261–62.
3   Lawrence E. Stager, "The Song of Deborah—Why Some Tribes Answered the Call and Others Did Not," *Biblical Archaeology Review* 15.1 (1989): 51–55, 57–59, 62–64, https://library.biblicalarchaeology.org/article/the-song-of-deborah-why-some-tribes-answered-the-call-and-others-did-not/.

Consider your real-life response if your employer were asking you to betray the morality of your God.

How do you respond if staying out of an argument is beneficial for *you* but will abandon someone on the margins who can't fight for themselves?

What do you do if "keeping of the peace" maintains *your* standing at an institution or organization but allows the Christian identity of that institution to be compromised?

And what if the community you are serving has become corrupt? What would it take for you to step in and speak up?

What and who might you be betraying by choosing to stay out of the battle at hand?

Day 2: The Battle

First Contact

"An evil is coming that threatens our kingdom, our freedom. But we have a weapon they are not prepared for." These are the opening words to the trailer of *The Woman King*. The story is based on true events that took place in the 1820s in the kingdom of Dahomey on the West Coast of Africa. What was their weapon? The Agojie, an all-female group of elite warriors who were trained to "fear no one" and "to fear no pain" in defense of their homeland.

These women were often identified as superior to their male counterparts in both bravery and endurance and served Dahomey for over two hundred years. Why did they fight? In the words of actress Viola Davis, acting the part of the commanding officer of the Agojie, because "some things are worth fighting for."

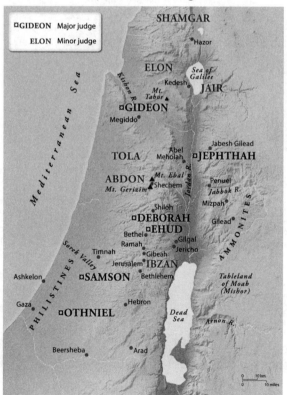

Map of Israel's Judges

Into the Book

Now that we know who Heber is, let's see what he's done. In this exercise you'll highlight the text and circle and draw lines on your map for both the good guys and bad guys. Be creative with this. Maybe use two colors (one for the bad guys and one for the good guys) or two styles of lines or another way that helps you best.

Read **Judges 4:12–16**.

¹² When they told Sisera that Barak son of Abinoam had gone up to Mount Tabor, ¹³ Sisera summoned from Harosheth Haggoyim to the Kishon River all his men and his nine hundred chariots fitted with iron.

¹⁴ Then Deborah said to Barak, "Go! This is the day the LORD has given Sisera into your hands. Has not the LORD gone ahead of you?" So Barak went down Mount Tabor, with ten thousand men following him. ¹⁵ At Barak's advance, the LORD routed Sisera and all his chariots and army by the sword, and Sisera got down from his chariot and fled on foot.

¹⁶ Barak pursued the chariots and army as far as Harosheth Haggoyim, and all Sisera's troops fell by the sword; not a man was left.

- Verse 12 begins with a plural pronoun as the subject, with no corresponding noun (antecedent) to go with the pronoun. Based on the context, who do you think "they" refers to?

- Highlight the name of the one who received the news about Barak.
- Underline what "they" told him.
- Circle on the map the place where Barak and his men are.
- Highlight what Sisera did as a result of the information given to him. Now circle on the map the place where Sisera's men were (remember that Harosheth Haggoyim is not shown on the map but is near Megiddo) and the place where they went. Draw a line connecting the two locations.
- Circle on the map where Barak and his men are located in verse 15.
- When Sisera and his men move out from Harosheth Haggoyim to the Kishon River, what command does Deborah, the prophet, give to Barak? Circle her command to Barak. Highlight the things that Deborah says the Lord has done.
- Take a minute and look back at session 5, day 1 and verses 6–7. Remember the plan? How do Yahweh's instructions there compare with what you see here in verses 13–14?

- Barak and his men begin at Mount Tabor. Draw a line on the map from there to the place where Barak and his men pursued the chariots and army.

- Highlight what Barak and his men did to Sisera's troops. Underline what Sisera did.
- Who does the battle belong to?

Real People, Real Places, Real Faith

"For any ancient commander, control of an army in battle was a virtual impossibility. Once the fog of war had descended, most generals had little influence on the outcome."[1] According to Deborah O'Daniell Cantrell, that "fog of war" was far worse when chariotry was involved.[2] If a horse was to succeed in navigating this chaos and remain functional as a weapon, if a chariot regiment was to succeed as the superweapons they were designed to be, the horses must be *thoroughly* trained. Noise, the vibration of the thundering wheels, clashing weaponry, shouting men—these could not make the horse panic. As a result, "the value of the seasoned war-horse may explain why the booty lists following battles almost always give horses first mention and appear to contain the exact numbers of captured horses."[3] Predictably, a regular strategy of chariot warfare was to attempt to panic the *enemies'* horses. There is in fact a classic tale about the chariotry of Thutmose III engaged against the forces of Megiddo. Recorded by one Amenemheb, an Eighteenth-Dynasty Egyptian army officer, the story reports that the Canaanites (Megiddo) intentionally let loose a mare who was "in season" onto the battlefield. The objective? To create mayhem among the stallions pulling the Egyptian chariots. And it worked! Whereas the Canaanite stallions' nostrils had been swabbed with a strong-smelling salve to mask the odor of the mare prior to the battle, the defenseless Egyptian stallions reportedly went mad, wreaking havoc among man and beast on the battlefield. Commander Amenemheb heroically corralled and executed the offending mare, freeing the stallions to get back to the business of battle![4] In the following verses, hear the biblical authors describe chariots in action. And note that both Barak and Lappidoth's names are associated with the same!

---

1   Simon Anglim et al., *Fighting Techniques of the Ancient World 3000 BC–AD 500: Equipment, Combat Skills, and Tactics* (New York: Thomas Dunne Books St. Martin's Press, 2002), 135.
2   Deborah O'Daniell Cantrell, *The Horsemen of Israel: Horses and Chariotry in Monarchic Israel* (Ninth–Eighth Centuries B.C.E.) (Winona Lake, IN: Eisenbrauns, 2011), 27.
3   Cantrell, *Horsemen of Israel*, 34.
4   Cantrell, *Horsemen of Israel*, 23.

Through the window peered Sisera's mother;
> behind the lattice she cried out,
"Why is his chariot so long in coming?
> Why is the *clatter* of his chariots delayed?" (Judg 5:28, emphasis added)

The shields of his soldiers are red;
> the warriors are clad in scarlet.
The *metal on the chariots flashes*
> on the day they are made ready;
> the spears of juniper are brandished.
The *chariots storm through the streets,*
> rushing back and forth through the squares.
They look *like flaming torches* [Lappidoth];
> they dart about *like lightning* [Barak]! (Nah 2:3–4, emphasis added)

Our People, Our Places, Our Faith

Let's pause to remember again that in the new covenant it is not military acquisition that expands the borders of the kingdom. The victories of the kingdom don't come through swords or armor or chariots. Rather, as Paul tells us in 2 Corinthians 10:3–4, "Though we live in the world, *we do not wage war* as the world does. The weapons we fight with are not the weapons of the world. On the contrary, they have divine power to demolish strongholds" (emphasis added). Thus, although you and I are entreated a number of times in the New Testament to behave as "good" or "fellow" soldiers (Phil 2:25; 2 Tim 2:3; Phlm v. 2), the armor we carry is the belt of truth, the breastplate of righteousness, the shield of faith, and the helmet of salvation (Eph 6:11–17). Why all this warrior talk? Because we *are* engaged in a war, just not one "against flesh and blood." Our war is against "the powers of this dark world and against the spiritual forces of evil in the heavenly realms" (Eph 6:12). Our orders are not to win *land* but to win *hearts* (and to defend hearts). You are I are called as *spiritual* warriors, "so that when the day of evil comes, you may be able to stand your ground, and after you have done everything, to stand" (v. 13).

Day 3: The Victory

First Contact

It was February 22, 1980, and most Americans were glued to their TV sets watching the Winter Olympic Games in Lake Placid, New York. It was the medal round of the men's hockey tournament. The United States versus the Soviet Union, and it was *huge*. What made it such a big deal? Well, for one, the United States and the USSR had been Cold War adversaries for over thirty years. That would be enough to explain the rivalry. But add to the mix that the Soviet team was made up of de facto professionals, whereas the American team, strictly enforcing the "amateur only" rules, was made up of twenty college-age guys with no professional experience. They were the youngest hockey team in US Olympic history. Add the fact the Soviet team had won *four consecutive gold medals* and since 1964 had outscored their opponents 175 to 44 . . . well, that's just too much. The Soviet team that year was widely claimed to be the best team in the world ever. The US team? Not so much.

Al Michaels got to call that game. And instead of the rout that everyone expected, Michaels witnessed what has come to be known as the "Miracle on Ice," the "top sports moment of the 20th century."[1] The US took the game, impossibly, 4–3! As the final seconds ticked away, the crowd went absolutely *insane*. Michaels shouted above the din, "Do you believe in miracles?! *Yes!* Unbelievable!" And then the very best part of all, the US players, barely more than boys, fell all over each other, jumping, laughing, crying, hugging, slapping, heads thrown back, smiles wide, tears flowing. Do you believe in miracles? Yes, you bet I do!

Into the Book

Exactly how does Barak and his ten thousand troops, mostly farmers and frontiersmen with homemade weapons, defeat Sisera's army of "nine hundred chariots fitted with iron"? If you

---

1   "The 1980 U.S. Olympic Team," U. S. Hockey Hall of Fame.com, https://www.ushockeyhalloffame.com/page/show/831562-the-1980-u-s-olympic-team.

recall from session 5, these chariots were mobile artillery platforms pulled by well-trained war-horses. They were manned with at least two men, one a driver and the other an archer. These machines were dreaded and deadly on dry, flat ground. It would take a miracle!

Papyrus showing Ramesses II fighting from his chariot
Copyright © 1995 by Phoenix Data Systems

Start with reading **Psalm 68:7–8**.

> ⁷ When you, God, went out before your people,
>   when you marched through the wilderness,
> ⁸ the earth shook, the heavens poured down rain,
>   before God, the One of Sinai,
>   before God, the God of Israel.

- In the verses, circle the names and titles of God.
- Using a different color, circle the nouns in verse 8, and highlight the verbs associated with those nouns.

• How does the writer present God in these verses? In other words, what do you think of when you read "went out before your people" and "marched through the wilderness"?

In the account of the battle in Judges 4, we get just the facts, but here in chapter 5 we get the details. Read **Judges 5:4–5, 19–21**.

> ⁴ "When you, Lord, went out from Seir,
>   when you marched from the land of Edom,
> the earth shook, the heavens poured,
>   the clouds poured down water.
> ⁵ The mountains quaked before the Lord, the One of Sinai,
>   before the Lord, the God of Israel.
>
> ¹⁹ "Kings came, they fought,
>   the kings of Canaan fought.
> At Taanach, by the waters of Megiddo,
>   they took no plunder of silver.
> ²⁰ From the heavens the stars fought,
>   from their courses they fought against Sisera.
> ²¹ The river Kishon swept them away,
>   the age-old river, the river Kishon.
>   March on, my soul; be strong!"

• Compare verses 4 and 5 from Judges with verses 7 and 8 from the Psalms passage. Circle and highlight verses 4 and 5 in the Judges passage the same as you did in the Psalms passage. Who is leading the Israelite army?

- When the Lord marched out ahead of the Israelites (v. 4) what did he bring with him? What did he cause to happen?

- As a result of what happened in verse 4, what happened to the Kishon River (v. 21)?

- In session 1, day 3 you heard about Baal, one of the Canaanite gods. He is the god of fertility and storm. He is often portrayed holding a thunderbolt. How did Yahweh defeat Sisera and his army? Who was the true opponent in this battle?

Real People, Real Places, Real Faith

In our study today we have been interacting primarily with Judges 5, the epic poem that retells the great story of Deborah and Barak. The epigraphists (the experts in studying inscriptions) agree that this is one of the oldest pieces of poetry in the entire Bible. And it is indeed an "epic." An epic is defined as "a long narrative poem that relates the great deeds of a larger-than-life hero who embodies the values of a particular society and upon whom the fate of his people depend."[2] The elements that typically distinguish epics include "superhuman deeds, fabulous adventures, highly stylized language, and a blending of lyrical and dramatic traditions."[3]

Can you see all of this in Judges 5? I can! The poem is long and tells a tale. Our larger-than-life characters now include Deborah, Barak, Sisera, and Jael! Which ones embody the values of Israelite society? The unflinching covenant confidence of Deborah, the equally unflinching courage of Barak, and Jael's choice of Yahweh over every other alliance in her life. Not only do we have a true epic here (think Homer's *Odyssey*, *Beowulf*, the Lord of the Rings) but we also have some strong parallels to another epic poem in the Bible, the Song of the Sea in Exodus

---

2   Quizlet, s.v. "epic," accessed May 20, 2024, https://quizlet.com/522309490/epic-poem-epic-hero-flash-cards/.
3   Poets.org, s.v. "epic," accessed April 23, 2024, https://poets.org/glossary/epic.

15. In both, the people of God stand on the other side of sure disaster and are overcome with praise for their miraculous deliverance from the enemies. And how interesting it is that in both epic poems, which shape the destiny of a nation, the miracle that delivers the people is the divine manipulation of . . . water. For the children of Abraham trapped between Pharaoh's chariots and the Red Sea, the faith of Moses and the miracle power of the Almighty *parted the Red Sea*. Impossible. For the tribes of Israel trapped between Sisera's chariots and Mount Tabor, the faith of Deborah and the miracle power of the Almighty *flooded the Kishon River*. Impossible. "The river Kishon swept them away, the age-old river, the river Kishon. March on, my soul; be strong!" (Judg 5:21). As Daniel Block says, "Whereas the extrabiblical odes tend to represent hyperbolic celebrations of superhuman achievements, Exodus 15 and Judges 5 overflow with praise to God."[4]

Our People, Our Places, Our Faith

Do you believe in miracles? I do. I've seen too many *not* to believe. But here's what I don't like about miracles—they never show up until there's no way back. Keep in mind that not one of those men waiting in the dark on the backside of Mount Tabor had any idea that God was planning a thunderstorm. Not one of them who charged wholeheartedly down the slopes of Tabor into the firestorm ahead knew the Kishon was about to flood. Not a single person who said yes that day knew how this thing would end. But they answered the call anyway. Do you believe in miracles? I do. But sometimes I wish they were a bit less, well, miraculous.

---

4 Daniel Block, "Judges," *Zondervan Illustrated Bible Backgrounds commentary*, vol. 2 (Grand Rapids: Zondervan, 2009), 144.

Day 4: Meet the Judges

Samson

> ### 12
>
> ### Samson
>
> **Meaning of name:** "Yahweh is (my) sun"
>
> **Family background:** Father Manoah, mother unnamed; from the tribe (clan) of the Danites
>
> **Title given:** A Nazarite, dedicated to God from the womb
>
> **Israel's disobedience:** Did evil in the eyes of the Lord
>
> **Empowerment:** The Spirit of the Lord
>
> **Oppressor:** Philistines
>
> **Length of oppression:** Forty years
>
> **Length of peace:** Peace not mentioned, but Samson led twenty years

First Contact

Songs have been written about him. Movies have been made about him. His strength is unmatched by anyone else in the Old Testament. His wife's name is as well-known as his. The Bible provides more information about his background than any other judge in the book of Judges. A razor never touches his head (until the end of his story). Whereas the first judge of Israel, Othniel, was the most exemplary judge, Samson, the final judge presented in the cycle, is the least exemplary judge and one of the most tragic found in the book. Before his birth the angel of the Lord announced to Samson's mother that she would give birth to a son who would be "dedicated to God from the womb" and would "take the lead in delivering Israel from the hands of the Philistines" (Judg 13:5).

Reading & Observing

Map of Israel's Judges

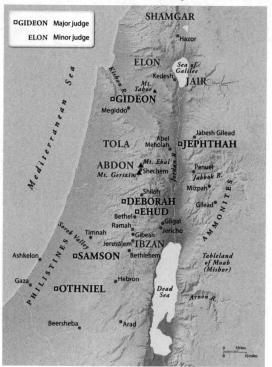

- Find **Samson** on the map and circle his name.
- Complete the Samson column in the following table.

Cycle found in Judges 2:11–19	Samson (Judges 13–16)
Israelites did evil in the eyes of the Lord	13:1
They served other gods, forsook the Lord	
They aroused the Lord's anger	
The Lord gave them/sold them into the hands of raiders/enemies	13:1
The people groaned under the oppression; cried out to the Lord	
The Lord raised up judges who saved them	13:5
When the judge died, the people returned to following other gods	
Oppressor	13:5
Length of peace	
Death notice	16:30

Turn in your Bible to **Judges 14:1–4** and answer the following questions.

- Who does Samson want his father to get him for a wife? Where was she from?

- What is wrong with this picture? What had the Israelites been commanded regarding intermarrying?

- Who was "ruling over Israel" at that time?

• What was God's purpose (v. 4)?

What we see through much of the rest of the Samson story is Samson seeking revenge against the Philistines for wrongs done to him by them. And the Philistines are seeking ways to destroy their enemy, Samson. When you have time, read through his whole story. For now we're going to highlight a few things.

• For each of these references, write down the wrong that was done to Samson and Samson's response.

15:1–5

15:6–8

15:9–15

Until this point, there has been one mention of Samson being a judge. That is found in **Judges 13:5** when the angel of the Lord tells Samson's mother that "he will take the lead in delivering Israel from the hands of the Philistines."

Now look at **15:18–20**. Just prior to this, Samson had killed one thousand men with a jawbone.

[18] Because he was very thirsty, he cried out to the LORD, "You have given your servant this great victory. Must I now die of thirst and fall into the hands of the uncircumcised?" [19] Then God opened up the hollow place in Lehi, and water came out of it. When Samson drank, his strength returned and he revived. So the spring was called En Hakkore, and it is still there in Lehi.

[20] Samson led Israel for twenty years in the days of the Philistines.

- In verse 18, what does Samson acknowledge that Yahweh has done?

- How long did Samson lead Israel?

Among one of the most popular judge stories is that of Samson and Delilah. As the story goes, the Philistine rulers promised to pay Delilah if she would find out the source of Samson's strength so that they could overpower and subdue him. After tiring of Delilah's nagging, Samson gives in and tells her. The Philistine rulers come in and give Delilah her silver. Samson, not realizing that the Lord has left him, falls into the hands of the Philistines, who gouge out his eyes and put him in prison grinding grain. When the Philistines are offering sacrifices and praising their god Dagon for giving them victory over Samson, they bring Samson out to make a spectacle of him. In one last act of vengeance, Samson prays to Yahweh for strength (16:28) and brings down the temple of Dagon on him and the Philistines, killing "many more [Philistines] when he died than while he lived" (16:30).

Responding: What's Your Territory?

In this week's individual lessons we met Heber the traitor, saw the battle unfold, and witnessed Yahweh's victory. In looking at the last major judge in the book of Judges, we saw a man who was called from the womb and had such potential yet made some bad choices.

How are you doing with journaling?

- What territory can you see from where you're standing that belongs to the kingdom of God and, for whatever reason, is not yet in the hand of God's people?

- Is it worth fighting for?

- What are you going to do about it?

SESSION 7

Deborah's Battle
and Victory

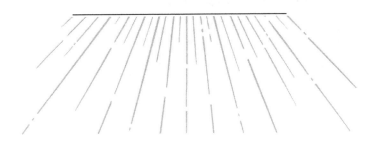

SESSION 7: GROUP MEETING

Schedule

GROUP MEETING

Session 7 Video Teaching and Discussion

INDIVIDUAL STUDY

Day 1: Jael and Sisera

Day 2: Sisera's Mother

Day 3: The Reckoning

Day 4: Meet the Judges—Deborah

Getting Started

Leader, open your group with these icebreaker questions.

- Is anyone here in the military? Married to someone in the military? The child of a military family?
- Has anyone here seen live combat?
- Tell us what makes the military life and military people unique.

Watch Session 7 Video: Deborah's Battle and Victory [25 Minutes]

Streaming video access instructions are on the inside front cover of each study guide.

Video Outline

Follow along during the video, take notes, or write down questions and aha moments as you like.

I. The traitor: Heber the Kenite

    A. Who are the Kenites?

    B. What is Heber doing?

        1. The separation

        2. The betrayal

II. The battle: Go time!

   A. "They" told Sisera Barak's location

   B. Sisera summoned his men to the Kishon River

   C. Deborah commands Barak to go!

   D. Victory from Yahweh

III. The victory: How?

   A. Who caused the rain?

   B. What was Baal's thing?

   C. Who was the true opponent?

IV. The Song of Deborah

Dialogue, Digest & Do

Discuss the following as a group.

- Before this lesson, had you even heard of Heber the Kenite? What did you learn about him?

- When Barak's men realized they had been sold out, what were the first emotions that flooded through camp? Have you ever been in that space? If you feel comfortable, describe that sense of betrayal to the group.

- What emotions flooded your heart when you heard Deborah's response to the "all is lost" moment—check verse 14 again.

- What changed for you when you heard Deborah and Barak in our epic poem reading in the video?

- Sandy offered us Théoden at the siege of Gondor and the last battle of *Braveheart* as her comparisons of the battle of Mount Tabor. Which battle scene would you compare it to?

- When the men of Zebulun and Naphtali came rushing down the slopes of Mount Tabor, with brave Barak at their head and Deborah perched above the battlefield with eyes of steel, *did anyone have any idea that the Kishon was going to flood?* Did they know the chariots would be rendered useless and, at the moment of the flood, they would be the ones on the basalt bridge? Who could've known? Only Yahweh. What if Deborah and Barak had not obeyed?

- Now that you know it is Baal who supposedly brings the rain, how does that make this story even better?

Next Week

Four more days of homework! Complete all four days before our final meeting. We'll be discussing Jael, Sisera, Sisera's mother, and the tribes that didn't show up.

Closing Prayer

Leader, ask your group members if there is anything they would like prayer for, especially something highlighted by this week's video.

Israel's Promised Tribal Allotments

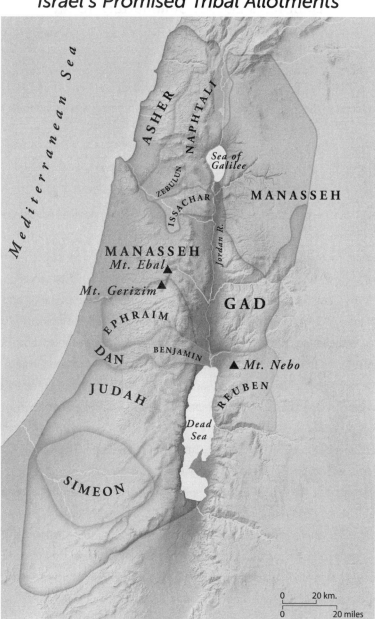

Deborah's Legacy Still Matters Today

The lessons found in the individual studies focus on the *upcoming* week's video lecture.

A Word from Sandy

When we left our heroes, they had just accomplished the impossible. A volunteer militia, a courageous captain, and a steely-eyed prophet transformed twenty years of profound loss into an unimaginable moment of victory. God spoke. The people answered. The enemy charged. And, astonishingly, an unexpected solution burst onto the scene! This military moment should have been a rout, but because of the faith of Deborah, the courage of Barak, and the loyalty of the good men of Zebulun and Naphtali, this moment changed the trajectory of a generation. As I say in the video, "Courage and integrity and allegiance to the covenant color every corner of this scene." But as any military strategist would tell us—on paper, Israel's chances for success were slim at best. Not only were Barak's forces outgunned, but the untimely betrayal of a supposed ally robbed Barak of the element of surprise and forced him to move before he intended. But miraculously in this "all is lost" moment, as our heroes were rushing the Black Gate of Mordor, it began to rain. I love that. Such a simple solution! The Kishon River flooded, the playing field was leveled, and the people of God took the day!

So how might this "story that matters" speak into our new-covenant hearts today? Well, for starters, this story has me thinking about mustard seeds and leaven. Do you remember Matthew 13:31–33, where Jesus tries to explain the strategy of the kingdom to his disciples? They expect Jesus to lead a military coup, a violent revolution against the Roman Empire, but he instead says the kingdom is like the smallest seed in the garden, which produces the largest plant. He also compares it to the invisible inclusion of yeast in flour, which with a little warmth and wet transforms the entire lump of dough. Indeed, the strategy of victory for the kingdom of God in *both* covenants is that God delights in choosing "the weak things of the world to shame the strong" (1 Cor 1:27). Feeling a little outgunned today? You might be exactly where God wants you.

Day 1: Sisera and Jael

Real Time & Space

One of our best resources for studying the pastoral lifestyle of early Israel is to study the pastoral lifestyle of the Bedouin populations found in Lebanon, Israel, Jordan, Palestine, and the Sinai. Like Heber and Jael, the Bedouin are (or were) mobile pastoralists, living in large black tents made of goat hair. The shape of these tents is usually rectangular. The size varies—but 40' × 20' is normative. Because of the animal textiles they are made of (wool and hair), and their size, these tents are *really* heavy and take a team of several adults to set up and tear down. The tent stakes I know are about 18" long, but my experience is with desert Bedouin, and their tent pegs might be longer, as they are driving stakes into sand as opposed to the soil of the hill country. But generally, the bigger the tent, the longer the stake.

When you step inside one of these Bedouin tents, your first thought is how much difference shade makes in such a climate. You can feel and *smell* the life of the pastoralist all around you, and during the daytime you can see the pinpricks of sunlight peeking through the warp and weave of the heavy cloth. In the modern period, these tents are usually divided into two sections—one for men and one for women. The men's side is dedicated to hospitality—the public sphere. The women's side is dedicated to domestic tasks—the private sphere. Most scholars think that this gender-divided space emerged with Islam in the seventh century CE, so we have no reason to conclude that the biblical era had divided tents. *But* we are clear that the larger family compounds of the biblical era had a number of tents, and a household with several wives might have had a tent for each wife and her children (see Gen 31:33). So we can predict that some tents were dedicated to hospitality, and some (likely women's) to domestic life. It is likely then that Sisera is taking refuge in Jael's tent and that the blanket she places over him is made of Awassi wool (also *very* heavy and very warm). Considering Heber's alliance with Jabin, the expectations of hospitality, and the fact that Jabin is a warrior and Jael a mere woman, Sisera has every reason to consider himself safe in this space.

Last thing: Know that the women who inhabited this world were strong and tough. Typically it was the women who took care of the setup and teardown of the family compound.[1] They also grazed the flocks, sheared the sheep, and roped and milked the herds. And all this in addition to weaving, cooking, frequent pregnancies, and raising children. And because pastoral households are mobile—the Bedouin move twice a year on average, once in the summer and once in the spring—there was a lot of setting up and tearing down going on! All told, our girl Jael knew *exactly* what to do with a hammer and a tent peg, and she had a lot of practice doing it.

First Contact

Do you remember the Disney princess film *Tangled*? My favorite fairy-tale flick! In my mind, it was the first time a Disney *prince* got to do more than serve as a backdrop for the dress. But best, this one came out when my princesses were tiny, and every time we watched it (that would be somewhere around 2,472 times), when the credits started rolling and "Something That I Want" started playing, we would crank the volume, and my freshly scrubbed, bed-bound little princesses and I would jump up off the couch and dance all over our living room singing at the top of our lungs. Ah, those were the days! And my favorite trope in that awesome little flick? That would be the frying pan . . .

Into the Book

You saw this table a few sessions ago. Today you can complete the information for the players to be named later (that would be Heber and Jael)! Note: Table key on p. 213.

---

1   Suzanne Ezzat Joseph, "Forms of Production and Demographic Regimes: An Anthropological Demographic Study of Bedouin Agro-Pastoral Tribes in the Bekaa Valley, Lebanon" (PhD diss., The University of Georgia, 2002).

Name	Title	Good guy or bad guy?	Meaning of name*
Ehud (3:15; 4:1)	deliverer; the son of Gera the Benjaminite	Good	"where is majesty"
Jabin (4:2)	king of Canaan who reigned in Hazor	Bad	Canaanite name; something like "he will establish understanding" or "may he be wise"†
Sisera (4:2)	the commander of Jabin's army	Bad	Not a Semitic name (not Canaanite, not Hebrew); probably a Philistine name; meaning uncertain
Deborah (4:4)	prophet, wife of Lappidoth	Good	"Yahweh leads," or "may Yahweh lead"
Lappidoth (4:4)	husband of Deborah	Good	customary meaning is "torches" but also means "lightning"
Barak (4:6)	son of Abinoam; commander of the Israelite army	Good	"lightning"
Heber (1:16; 4:11, 17)			in modern Hebrew often used to mean "a close friend"; in biblical Hebrew possibly associated with Hebron; related to the Amorite word meaning "tribe" or "clan"; in Mari it "refers to a nomadic unit that has not yet settled down"‡
Jael (4:17; 5:24–27)			mountain goat

* See Richard S. Hess, "Israelite Identity and Personal Names from the Book of Judges," *Hebrew Studies* 44 (2003): 25–39; Hess, "The Name Game: Dating the Book of Judges," *Biblical Archeology Review* 30 (2004): 38–41; Sasson, *Judges 1–12*; Stone, *Judges*.
† Richter's translation.
‡ See Hess, "Name Game"; Sasson, *Judges*, 262.

Now read **Judges 4:17–21**.

¹⁷ Sisera, meanwhile, fled on foot to the tent of Jael, the wife of Heber the Kenite, because there was an alliance between Jabin king of Hazor and the family of Heber the Kenite.

¹⁸ Jael went out to meet Sisera and said to him, "Come, my lord, come right in. Don't be afraid." So he entered her tent, and she covered him with a blanket.

¹⁹ "I'm thirsty," he said. "Please give me some water." She opened a skin of milk, gave him a drink, and covered him up.

²⁰ "Stand in the doorway of the tent," he told her. "If someone comes by and asks you, 'Is anyone in there?' say 'No.'"

²¹ But Jael, Heber's wife, picked up a tent peg and a hammer and went quietly to him while he lay fast asleep, exhausted. She drove the peg through his temple into the ground, and he died.

- Where did Sisera run to? Whose tent is it? Does that surprise you? (cf. Gen 31:33)

- What reason is given for Sisera fleeing to Heber's family?

- In reading verse 18, what do you think Jael's intentions were?

- What does Sisera ask for in verse 19? What does Jael give him instead?

- Who do you suppose was the someone Sisera was expecting to come by the tent?

- I love how verse 21 begins: "But Jael . . ." Rather than going and standing in the doorway, what did Jael do?

- The reader gets no help with how Jael is feeling. She just drove a tent peg through a guy's skull, and all the narrator says is, "And he died." What thoughts do you imagine going through Jael's mind?

- List three things that make Jael an unlikely hero.

Now read **Judges 5:24–27**.

> ^{24} "Most blessed of women be Jael,
>   the wife of Heber the Kenite,
>   most blessed of tent-dwelling women.
> ^{25} He asked for water, and she gave him milk;
>   in a bowl fit for nobles she brought him curdled milk.
> ^{26} Her hand reached for the tent peg,
>   her right hand for the workman's hammer.
> She struck Sisera, she crushed his head,
>   she shattered and pierced his temple.
> ^{27} At her feet he sank,
>   he fell; there he lay.
> At her feet he sank, he fell;
>   where he sank, there he fell—dead."

- How does the poet depict Jael in these verses?

Real People, Real Places, Real Faith

Let's look at Jael for a moment. What do we know about her? She is a woman. She is a pastoralist. She is the wife of Heber, a Kenite, a descendant of Moses's brother-in-law. That means she is an outsider. Not quite a foreigner, but someone who via fictive kinship has been assimilated into the tribe of Judah as a client of sorts (see Judg 1:16). We also know that her husband is a traitor. First he breaks his alliance with the tribe of Judah, moving to Kedesh in Naphtali. Then he forges an alliance with Israel's oppressor, Jabin. Jael is also a pastoralist living among agriculturalists. It might help to think of the long-standing conflicts in our own American West between the ranchers and the farmers. Jael is not a judge or a warrior and likely is not well known or well liked among her Israelite neighbors. A hero? Unlikely. She certainly knows of the covenant her husband has made with Jabin, and there is no indication in the text that she is surprised to see Sisera at her tent asking for aid. Although she knows of the covenant her husband made, she apparently does not agree with his choice. So what is *her* choice? Jael chooses the purposes of the God of Israel. She decides that the purposes of the God of Israel are her purposes. The enemy of God is her enemy. And she utilizes *domestic* space and *domestic* tools to advance the kingdom. Does she *need* to be a warrior or a judge to do her part? No.

Our People, Our Places, Our Faith

How are you doing with identifying the territory that you can see from where you're standing that you know belongs to the kingdom of God and, for whatever reason, is not yet in the hands of God's people?

Sometimes, as is the case with Jael, that territory (or that person) walks right into the front door of your tent. But even Jael had a choice. Was she going to do the easy thing and keep Sisera (and her husband) happy? Or was she going to fight for her true allegiance?

Are there any spaces in your life right now where you share Jael's dilemma? Where do you have choices to make? What will it take for you to make them?

How will making these choices define where your allegiance lies?

Day 2: Sisera's Mother

First Contact

Do you remember the scene from *The Hunger Games* when Katniss is summoned to the war room? Her task is to demonstrate to the sponsors that she has what it takes to be a contender. She is more than off-balance. A week ago she was just a girl from a coal-mining town in District 12. Now she is supposed to be a warrior. The sponsors hardly notice her entrance. They're enjoying an embarrassment of exotic food and drink, and the hushed conversations of the privileged inhabits the elegantly furnished balcony above. Katniss tries to hold it together. She selects a bow from the weapons rack. An arrow next. The sponsors quiet their revelry to watch her. She aims, she fires, she *misses*. The sponsors laugh—she was exactly what they expected. She grabs another arrow, aims, fires, *bull's-eye!* But the sponsors have lost interest by now—who expects anything from a girl from District 12? You remember what happens next. One more arrow, one more target, and the sponsors . . . well, *now* they're paying attention.

Into the Book

Read **Judges 5:28–31**. Here we meet the third woman in the story of Deborah, the nameless character of Sisera's mother.

> ²⁸ "Through the window peered Sisera's mother;
>   behind the lattice she cried out,
> 'Why is his chariot so long in coming?
>   Why is the clatter of his chariots delayed?'
> ²⁹ The wisest of her ladies answer her;
>   indeed, she keeps saying to herself,
> ³⁰ 'Are they not finding and dividing the spoils:
>   a woman or two for each man,

colorful garments as plunder for Sisera,
    colorful garments embroidered,
highly embroidered garments for my neck—
    all this as plunder?"

[31] "So may all your enemies perish, LORD!
    But may all who love you be like the sun
    when it rises in its strength."

Then the land had peace forty years.

- What is Sisera's mother doing when the reader meets her? What verbs are used for her actions?

- Look in other Bible translations and list at least three ways in which "cried out" (v. 28) is rendered.

- The "window" in verse 28 would not be a glass-paned window but rather an open hole in the wall for light and air. The "lattice" would be similar. Look at the questions she asks in the second half of the verse. Rewrite her questions in your own words.

- What picture do you get of his mother from the portrayal in verse 28?

- We learned in 4:2 that Sisera was based in Harosheth Haggoyim, which is near Megiddo. Based on the questions that Sisera's mother asks in the second half of verse 28, where do you think she is located?

- In verses 29 and 30, what do the ladies and she keep telling themselves? Highlight the things they name as spoils or plunder.

- Verse 31 is reminiscent of the Psalms. Often in the Psalms the psalmist cries out to Yahweh regarding the fate of their enemies. Here is one example. Read **Psalm 92:9, 12–13**.

> ⁹ For surely your enemies, Lord,
>   surely your enemies will perish. . . .
>
> ¹² The righteous will flourish like a palm tree,
>   they will grow like a cedar of Lebanon;
> ¹³ planted in the house of the Lord,
>   they will flourish in the courts of our God.

Real People, Real Places, Real Faith

Every soldier is someone's son. And any mother worth her salt would be worried when her son is delayed returning home from battle. Such a delay would have any of us checking our phone, staring out the window, getting antsy. In Judges 5:28 we feel Sisera's mother's pain. She's worried. I'd be worried too! She watched the men ride out at dawn—the prancing, snorting warhorses galloping out with their gilded iron chariots clattering behind. The proud captains in their bright colors and armor blazing in the sun. The shields and bows and arrows and banners. She'd heard the war horns calling out the command to ride. And she'd been proud of her son, tall and commanding and in charge, driving his captain's chariot at the front of the unit. And she had smiled and waved and cheered as Sisera's fighting force had ridden through the city gates, cantering across the fields, fanning out across the valley in perfect formation. "He'll be back by the evening meal," she thought as she turned away from her window. And under normal conditions, she would have been right. But in this case, her son has chosen to do battle with the living God. And the workforce that has kept Sisera's mother living in luxury and comfort?

They are the oppressed people of that same living God. Sisera has significantly underestimated his opponent. His mother has chosen the blindness born of privilege. Similar to the citizens of the Capital in *The Hunger Games*, Sisera's mother is about to get a wake-up call.

Our People, Our Places, Our Faith

As we come to the end of this "story that matters," quite unusual to biblical narrative, we realize that this story has always been about three *women*. One of these women draws our admiration as someone we want to emulate. She is a leader's leader: she has integrity, courage, steadfast conviction. Her voice is heard in the boardroom. She's a CEO willing to risk the fears of her constituency and move them forward to their true objectives. One of these women shows up as what my field hockey coach would have called a "sleeper"—an unexpected hero. She certainly doesn't *look* like a contender, but now everyone in the audience knows her name. Where did she dig up the courage to assassinate a warlord in her kitchen? The third woman is everything we despise about wealth and influence. She is unaware, unconcerned, insulated from the suffering of others, and completely self-absorbed. The slaughter of ten thousand Israelites and the rape of their women have no impact on her . . . as long as she gets her dyed and embroidered garments when her son gets home. Folks, we're being told this story for a reason. It demands a response.

What question is the narrator asking?

Which of these women do *you* want to be? Why?

What needs to change in your life, in your posture toward the kingdom, in your posture toward yourself, for you to be more like one of the unlikely heroes or heroines of the book of Judges?

Day 3: The Reckoning

First Contact

When interviewed about her casting choices in *Wonder Woman*, the director explained her selection of Robin Wright as Antiope, the commanding general of the all-female, elite Amazon fighting force: "I needed someone who seems under control and is not overly aggressive, but who is truly a badass."[1] Hmm . . . I wonder if that is what the Almighty said when it was time to choose Deborah?

Into the Book

Judges 5:15–18 is a bit like a roll call of the tribes who showed up and those who didn't. First let's look one more time at **Judges 4:6**.

Israel's Promised Tribal Allotments

> ⁶She sent for Barak son of Abinoam from Kedesh in Naphtali and said to him, "The LORD, the God of Israel, commands you: 'Go, take with you ten thousand men of Naphtali and Zebulun and lead them up to Mount Tabor.'"

- In the verse, highlight the names of the tribes that Barak takes with him to Mount Tabor. Find those territories on the map provided and highlight those as well.

1 "Interview: Director Patty Jenkins on Bringing Wonder Woman to Cinema Screens," TheHollywoodNews .com, June 1, 2017, https://www.thehollywoodnews.com/2017/06/01/interview-director-patty-jenkins-bringing -wonder-woman-cinema-screens/.

- Now read **Judges 5:15–18**. In the passage, highlight the names of the tribes who showed up in one color and those who didn't show up in another. On the map, find the territories of those who didn't show up, and shade them in a color different from the one in the previous step (color 1: showed up; color 2: no show).

> ¹⁵ The princes of Issachar were with Deborah;
>> yes, Issachar was with Barak,
>>> sent under his command into the valley.
>
> In the districts of Reuben
>> there was much searching of heart.
> ¹⁶ Why did you stay among the sheep pens
>> to hear the whistling for the flocks?
> In the districts of Reuben
>> there was much searching of heart.
> ¹⁷ Gilead stayed beyond the Jordan.
>> And Dan, why did he linger by the ships?
> Asher remained on the coast
>> and stayed in his coves.
> ¹⁸ The people of Zebulun risked their very lives;
>> so did Naphtali on the terraced fields.

- Underline in the text what the tribes who were no-shows did instead of joining the battle. Why do you think they stayed home?

Real People, Real Places, Real Faith

Judges 5 tells us that the tribes of Reuben, Gilead (Gad), Dan, and Asher ignored the call to arms. Rather than defending their kinsmen, they stayed out of it and stayed at home. With the words of Moses and Joshua ringing in their ears, why would they do that? Larry Stager, in his article "The Song of Deborah—Why Some Tribes Answered the Call and Others Did Not," provides some insight. The tribes of Reuben and Gad were on the other side of the Jordan, living and working as pastoralists (see Num 32:1; Judg 5:16). As shepherds, they depended on trade with the local urban centers for survival. In other words, they were far enough away that it wasn't hard to convince themselves that the battle for the Jezreel Valley did not really affect them. And offending their trade partners, well, that might put them in a bad spot. As for Dan and Asher, they stayed "by the ships" and "remained on the coast" (Judg 5:17). Stager proposes that the men of Dan were actually serving as clients to the patron Phoenician shipping companies, kind of like subcontractors. And offending the shipping companies, well, that wouldn't go well on the golf course. Stager also points out that Asher's location on the coast likely meant the Asherites were working as seamen and longshoremen for the Canaanites on the coast. In sum, Reuben, Gad, Dan, and Asher ignored Deborah's call because they "had ties to non-Israelites that proved stronger than those that bound them to their tribal confederation."[2] In our language? These tribes' first alliance was not to Israel or to Israel's God.

Our People, Our Places, Our Faith

Let's take a moment to put ourselves in Reuben's shoes. Your church is debating a core issue of its faith identity. You know the debate is important. You know that the people on the right side of the issue need support. You are very concerned about what will happen to your church if your community compromises its identity. But you hate conflict. And you *really* hate it when people are mad at you. So you keep your distance. You claim ignorance. You choose not to get involved.

Or maybe Dan's situation fits your circumstances. Your company is allying itself with people and positions you simply can't affirm. But if you spoke up in the board meeting, you could offend some powerful people, and that could damage your professional network. So you turn a blind eye. You keep your head down.

Or maybe it's Asher's situation that looks familiar. You are seeing some unjust hiring and promotion practices coming out of HR and Personnel. You can see the bias, see the damage it is doing to peoples' careers, and it really concerns you. But if you speak up, you could draw fire yourself. And maybe those same people would start coming after you. So you choose silence.

---

2 Lawrence E. Stager, "The Song of Deborah—Why Some Tribes Answered the Call and Others Did Not," *Biblical Archaeology Review* 15.1 (1989): 51–55, 57–59, 62–64, https://library.biblicalarchaeology.org/article/the-song-of-deborah-why-some-tribes-answered-the-call-and-others-did-not/.

Thinking through the scenario that most closely describes your life right now, if someone who loved you pointed out your silence, how would you explain why you "sat among the sheep-folds" in a moment of crisis?

In what ways does Deborah's and Barak's lives compel you toward a different course of action?

Day 4: Meet the Judges

Deborah (and Her Team)

4

Deborah

Meaning of name: "Yahweh leads" or "may he
lead"

Family background: Wife of Lappidoth; held
court in the hill country of Ephraim

Title given: Prophet, judge, wife, mother

Israel's disobedience: Did evil in the eyes of
the Lord

Oppressor: Jabin and Sisera

Length of oppression: Twenty years

Length of peace: Forty years

Other information: Only female judge; had a
tree named after her

Her team:

Barak: "Lightning," son of Abinoam,
from Kedesh in Naphtali; courageous
commander of the Israelite army

Jael: "mountain goat," wife of Heber the Kenite;
loyal to Yahweh; tent-peg-wielding hero

**Ten thousand men from Zebulun and
Naphtali who willingly risked their lives**

First Contact

Here we are at the last of our day 4 studies. And here at last, the final character card goes to . . . Deborah and her team: Barak, Jael, and ten thousand unnamed men!

> Deborah: Our hero for this study, whose story encourages, inspires, and challenges us to do the hard thing, to say yes even when the cost is high.
>
> Barak: Military commander of the Israelite army who received a war oracle from Yahweh, trusted the word of Yahweh through the prophet, and led ten thousand men into battle.
>
> Jael: An unlikely hero, whose loyalty to her God and his covenant outweighed any other loyalties.
>
> Ten thousand unnamed men from Zebulun and Naphtali.

Reading & Observing

Fill in the missing information in the Deborah column on the table on pp. 198–199.

Responding: What's Your Territory?

In our final week of studying Deborah, some unlikely heroes, and the book of Judges, spend some time in prayer before your final responses to our consistent quest for personal application of this incredible story, which is also *our* story. May the Lord bless you and keep you as you return often to these questions and mark out new territories to be conquered for the kingdom!

- What territory can you see from where you're standing that you know belongs to the kingdom of God and, for whatever reason, is not yet in the hand of God's people?

- Is it worth fighting for?

- What are you going to do about it?

Cycle found in Judges 2:11–19	Othniel (Judges 3:7–11)	Ehud (Judges 3:12–29)
Israelites did evil in the eyes of the Lord	3:7	3:12
They served other gods, forsook the Lord	3:7 Baals and Asherahs	none mentioned
They aroused the Lord's anger	3:8	not specifically stated
The Lord gave them/ sold them into the hands of raiders/ enemies	3:8 "sold them"	3:12 "gave Eglon power over them"
The people groaned under the oppression; cried out to the Lord	3:9	3:15
The Lord raised up judges who saved them	3:9 "raised up a deliverer"	3:15 "gave them a deliverer"
When the judge died, the people returned to following other gods	3:11, 12 "again they did evil"	4:1
Oppressor	3:8 Cushan-Rishathaim king of Aram Naharaim	3:12–13 Eglon king of Moab
Length of peace	3:11 forty years	3:30 eighty years
Other observations	"The Spirit of the LORD came upon him"	left-handed man; assassinated Eglon; struck down ten thousand Moabites; credited victory to Yahweh
Death notice	3:11	4:1

Deborah (Judges 4–5)	Gideon (Judges 6–8)	Jephthah (Judges 10:6–12:7)	Samson (Judges 13–16)
4:1	6:1	10:6	13:1
	6:10 gods of the Amorites	10:6 Baals, Ashtoreths, gods of Aram, the gods of Sidon, the gods of Moab, the gods of the Ammonites, and the gods of the Philistines	
	not specifically stated	10:7 he became angry with them	
4:2 "sold them"	6:1 "gave them into the hands of the Midianites"	10:7 "sold them"	13:1 "delivered them"
4:3	6:6	10:10, 15–16 cried out, "we have sinned"; "rescue us now"; got rid of the foreign gods	
4:4	3:14 "Go in the strength you have and save Israel"		13:5
	8:33		
4:2	6:1–6 Midianites	10:7–8 Ammonites and Philistines	13:5 Philistines
5:31	8:28 forty years		
		10:11–14; 11:29	
	8:28, 32, 33	12:7	16:30

SESSION 8

Deborah's Legacy Still Matters Today

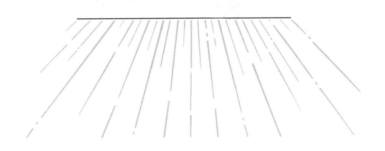

SESSION 8: GROUP MEETING

Getting Started

Leader, open your group with these icebreaker questions.

- Do you consider yourself a risk-taker? If yes, why? If not, what holds you back?
- For the folks in the crowd who *aren't* risk-takers, have you ever stepped out of that character trait and taken a risk, a big risk? What motivated you to step so far outside your comfort zone?

Watch Session 8 Video: Deborah's Legacy Still Matters Today [36 Minutes]

Streaming video access instructions are on the inside front cover of each study guide.

Video Outline

Follow along during the video, take notes, or write down questions and aha moments as you like.

I. What happened to Sisera? (Judg 4:16–22)

    A. Flees the battle on foot!

    B. Arrives at the family compound of Heber, his ally

C. Commands Jael to:

   1. Give him water (she gives him milk)

   2. Stand in the doorway and tell anyone who asks that no one is there

D. But Jael (v. 21)

   1. Drives a tent peg through Sisera's skull

   2. Shows Barak what she did

E. Yahweh subdued Jabin, Israelites destroyed him (v. 23)

II. Judges 5:24–27

A. "Most blessed of women be Jael" (v. 24)

B. "Shattered" and "pierced" warrior speak

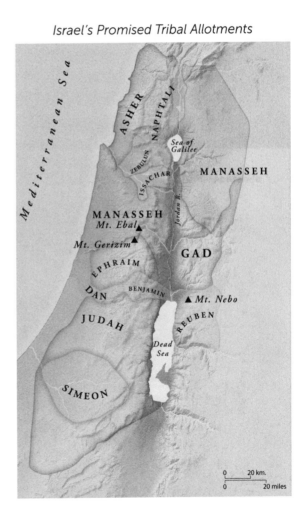

Israel's Promised Tribal Allotments

C. "This story extols the heroics of an ordinary person choosing the Lord's side and dramatizes the catalytic power of the prophetic word to elicit daring faithfulness."[1]

III. Sisera's mother

IV. The reckoning (5:15–18)

A. Who didn't show up?

1. Reuben

2. Gilead

3. Dan

4. Asher

B. Who showed up?

1. Ephraim

2. Benjamin

---

[1] Stone, *Judges*, 258.

3. Zebulun

4. Naphtali

5. Issachar

V. A story that matters: If the God of Deborah could bring victory to her, what might he do for you?

Dialogue, Digest & Do

Discuss the following as a group.

- You heard in the video that the stars in their courses fought against Sisera (Judg 5:20), and Sandy told us that "the message here is that Barak's battlefield was full of warriors that he could not see." Have you ever found yourself in that place? Have you been in a huge conflict, spent hours in preparatory prayer, and were trembling as you stepped forward in faith, but you could *feel* the presence of the Holy One fighting on your behalf? Tell the group about it.

- Talk about Jael for a moment. What did you learn about her that you did not know before?

- What was the most impactful aspect of this study for you and why?

- What makes Deborah's story a story that matters? Said another way, how might this very real past meet your very needy present? How might we reactualize this canon-worthy tale of courage and victory in the life of our church communities?

- As you think about Deborah's legacy, what is the legacy you hope to leave for generations to come?

Closing Prayer

In this final group prayer, offer a prayer over your group that each member would be willing to take the risk of fighting for that territory or territories they have identified throughout this study.

Sandy's prayer:

May the vision of Deborah and the courage of Barak and the willing hearts of the men of Naphtali be yours this day, and may we all find it in our hearts to build God's kingdom first.

Judges 5:2 in Sandy's words:

> When the *people of God* take the lead,
>> when the *people of God* willingly offer themselves—
>> praise the Lord!

Leader's Guide

This leader's guide is designed for you, the facilitator. If this is a home group, we recommend that an hour and a half be set aside for the video and discussion. If this is a group in a church setting, it can be modified to suit your group's schedule. In a perfect world, we recommend that the leader preview the videos. Outlines for each video session are provided for you and your group members in the "Video Outline" section in each week of the study.

Keep in mind that curriculum is a tool, not a straitjacket. You are the leader. You are called to lead this group. You can adjust according to your own style. But we also suggest that group members be allowed to talk, ask questions, offer aloud their aha moments and personal research. These elements are critical to the success of your group. Trust your group members, trust the Bible, trust the Holy Spirit, and let your people talk. Questions are provided to facilitate the discussion.

- Our prayer is that this material will give you the tools you need to successfully facilitate your group in your very own corner of the kingdom. Know that "where two or three gather in [Jesus's] name, there I am with them" (Matt 18:20). And know that the team behind this curriculum is praying daily that wherever you are, the Holy Spirit is with you. Godspeed!

FIRST THINGS

We are including here a few *suggestions* for the group's introductory meeting. You are welcome to plan this gathering in any way that best suits your group. Let the Holy Spirit be your guide.

- Make sure that the first gathering offers the group the opportunity to meet each other, get comfortable with one another, get the curriculum materials in hand, and get familiar with those materials.

- Keep in mind that hospitality is king! Allow the members of the group to briefly introduce themselves (i.e., first name and in one sentence what they hope to gain from this study). If the group has more than seven members, it is often good to have them turn to the person on their right and then on their left and introduce themselves before having everyone introduce themselves to the group as a whole. If this is a new group, know that "adult learning anxiety" is a very real thing. Expressions of hospitality such as snacks, music playing in the background, and a person or two assigned as host or hostess are all extremely helpful to lowering barriers and making newcomers feel at ease.

- Pass out materials and explain how the study works. Actually show them the various sections of a day's study. Make sure they are clear that the "homework" is to be completed *before* the video for each week. (The participants should work on individual study to session 1 at home prior to viewing the session 2 video at your next gathering, and so on.)

- Show your group the video streaming access instructions on the inside front cover of each study guide. This is a great tool for absences and re-viewing the teaching at any time.

- As you plan your schedule, it might also be a great thing to set apart a final gathering after the study is complete to debrief and celebrate with some sort of time together as a group.

PRACTICAL TIPS

- Choose a **space** for your study that matches the size of your group, facilitates note-taking, and encourages discussion.

- Have **refreshments**. A lot of studies have shown that adults do way better in small groups when snacks are available. For some reason, having a cup of coffee in their hand makes it easier for adults to speak to the person next to them. And if you pass snack responsibilities around, that gives everyone a chance to get involved.

- Have someone besides yourself serve as host/hostess (you've got enough to do) and think about having **name tags**. These are useful for helping folks engage someone they don't really know yet and breaking down barriers.

Each member of your group should receive a copy of *The Epic of Eden: Deborah Bible Study Guide*. The guide is intended to provide each participant with "homework" preparing them for the next group gathering where the video is presented. Note: There is no preparatory work for the first week's video teaching, but from that week forward there is individual homework to be done in the study guide to prepare for the next group meeting and video teaching session.

Each week in the study guide includes four sets of exercises—three days of study focused on Deborah and one day learning about another one of Israel's judges. Three or four slots of time per week to prepare this homework is a reasonable expectation—not too much, not too little. *Please* communicate to your group members that homework is *not* required.

There will be plenty to do and talk about in the group discussion time after the video teaching each week. This study is intended to help your members enter into inductive study of their Bibles while opening their minds to greater scholarship of the Bible without years of academic classroom work. I've done the heavy lifting and herein pass along the results! My hope is that I've included enough different learning styles that every member of your group will find themselves engaged and challenged. As long as your members feel this way, I've succeeded.

WEEKLY GROUP MEETING LINEUP

GETTING STARTED

This section offers a break-the-ice kind of question(s). The intent is to get your group thinking and lead into the video for the week.

WATCH SESSION VIDEO

Use streaming video or DVD. Each video will be approximately thirty minutes. Exact minutes are given in each session.

DIALOGUE, DIGEST & DO

This section consists primarily of questions for discussion based on the video. This is also a place for group members to ask questions about the homework and share something from the homework that captured their attention.

NEXT WEEK

This section provides a brief note about what is expected of the participants for the next session. I also provide a teaser about what is to come in the next session.

CLOSING PRAYER

This is the time to ask group members if there is anything for which they would like prayer and then close the session with prayer.

FORMAT OF THE WEEKLY
INDEPENDENT STUDY SECTION

- **A Word from Sandy.** Each week of individual home study commences with the introduction of the topic.
- **Real Time & Space.** This is a short section that situates the week's study in real time and context.
- **First Contact.** Each daily study begins with this section designed to get your members thinking about what is to come from their own real time and space.
- **Into the Book.** This is where the inductive Bible study begins in earnest. Our primary goal is to lead your group members into the discovery of the Bible. The questions direct students into a close reading of the text.
- **Real People, Real Places, Real Faith.** This section provides further information about the original setting of these biblical narratives and characters and challenges your group members to get back into the Bible's real time and space—to put themselves into the shoes of these not-so-ivory-tower heroes.
- **Our People, Our Places, Our Faith.** The final individual study section will bring the ancient story back into a contemporary setting. Respond to questions that draw modern associations to the biblical text and narrative.
- **Reading & Observing.** After the First Contact section in the day 4 studies, the Reading & Observing section provides passages to read concerning one of the other judges and asks questions to guide your observations.
- **Responding: What's Your Territory.** Here we present three questions that you will be asked every week in this study and provide you space to journal your progress as you move through the study.

Appendix 1

A Few Artists' Renderings of Deborah

Deborah, in a stained-glass window by the Russian-Jewish artist Marc Chagall, https://www
.biblicalarchaeology.org/daily/people-cultures-in-the-bible/people-in-the-bible/deborah-in
-the-bible/

Deborah, James Nesbit, 2017, https://jnesbit.com/products-2/deborah?rq=deborah

Deborah, Sara M. Novenson, Women of the Bible, Landscapes of the Soul, https://novenson.com
/product/deborah/

Deborah Judging Israel, Lee Oskar Lawrie, 1932, concrete, west-facing panel on the NW corner
of the building of the Nebraska state capitol, https://en.m.wikipedia.org/wiki/File:Nebraska
_State_Capitol_NW_corner_W_panel_1.JPG

Deborah Praises Jael, Gustave Doré, 1832–1883, https://www.artbible.info/art/large/213.html

Deborah's Victory Song, John Francis Bentley, stained glass, ca. late 1890s, https://loandbeholdbible
.com/2017/05/06/deborah-judges-israel-judges-44-10-51-31/

Icon of St. Deborah the Judge of Israel, https://www.uncutmountainsupply.com/icons/of-saints
/by-name/d-f/icon-of-st-deborah-the-judge-of-israel-english-1de05/

Jael, Deborah, and Barak, Salomon de Bray, 1597–1664, https://www.artbible.info/art/large/802.html

Appendix 2

Answer Keys

Session 1, Day 3 Table Key

1. Othniel; they forgot the Lord their God and served the Baals and the Asherahs
2. Ehud; they did evil in the eyes of the Lord, no specific sins listed
3. Shamgar; n/a
4. Deborah; they did evil in the eyes of the Lord, no specific sins listed
5. Gideon; they did evil in the eyes of the Lord, they worshiped the gods of the Amorites
6. Tola; n/a
7. Jair; n/a
8. Jephthah; they served the Baals and the Ashtoreths, and the gods of Aram, the gods of Sidon, the gods of Moab, the gods of the Ammonites and the gods of the Philistines; they no longer served the Lord
9. Ibzan; n/a
10. Elon; n/a
11. Abdon; n/a
12. Samson; they did evil in the eyes of the Lord

Session 7, Day 1 Table Key

Heber: the Kenite, descendant of Hobab, Moses's brother-in-law, made an alliance with Jabin; bad guy

Jael: wife of Heber the Kenite; good

Bibliography

Anglim, Simon, Phyllis G. Jestice, Rob S. Rice, Scott M. Rusch, and John Serrati. *Fighting Techniques of the Ancient World 3000 BC–AD 500: Equipment, Combat Skills, and Tactics.* New York: Thomas Dunne Books St. Martin's Press, 2002.

Block, Daniel. "Judges." *Zondervan Illustrated Bible Backgrounds commentary.* Vol. 2. Grand Rapids: Zondervan, 2009.

Borowski, Obed. *Agriculture in Iron Age Israel.* Boston: American Schools of Oriental Research, 2002.

Bush, George W. "Transcript of Bush Speech in Atlanta." CNN.com. November 8, 2011. http://edition.cnn.com/2001/US/11/08/rec.bush.transcript/.

Cantrell, Deborah O'Danielle. *The Horsemen of Israel: Horses and Chariotry in Monarchic Israel (Ninth–Eighth Centuries B.C.E.).* Winona Lake, IN: Eisenbrauns, 2011.

Cross, Frank Moore. *From Epic to Canon: History and Literature in Ancient Israel.* Baltimore: Johns Hopkins University Press, 1998.

Echevarria, II, Antulio J. "What Is Military Strategy?" *Military Strategy: A Very Short Introduction.* Very Short Introductions. New York: Oxford Academic, 2017; online ed. Oxford Academic, February 23, 2017. https://doi.org/10.1093/actrade/9780199340132.003.0001.

Hess, Richard S. "Israelite Identity and Personal Names from the Book of Judges." *Hebrew Studies* 44 (2003): 25–39.

———. "The Name Game: Dating the Book of Judges." *Biblical Archeology Review* 30 (2004): 38–41.

"Interview: Director Patty Jenkins on Bringing Wonder Woman to Cinema Screens." TheHollywoodNews.com, June 1, 2017. https://www.thehollywoodnews.com/2017/06/01 /interview-director-patty-jenkins-bringing-wonder-woman-cinema-screens/.

Joseph, Suzanne Ezzat. "Forms of Production and Demographic Regimes: An Anthropological Demographic Study of Bedouin Agro-Pastoral Tribes in the Bekaa Valley, Lebanon." PhD diss., The University of Georgia, 2002.

King, Philip J., and Lawrence E. Stager. *Life in Biblical Israel.* Louisville: Westminster John Knox, 2001.

Koehler, Ludwig, and Walter Baumgartner. *The Hebrew and Aramaic Lexicon of the Old Testament,* vol. 2. Leiden: Brill, 2001.

Mazar, Amihai. *Archaeology of the Land of the Bible 10,000–586 B.C.E.* New York: Doubleday, 1990.

Nissinen, Martti. *Prophets and Prophecy in the Ancient Near East.* Atlanta: Society of Biblical Literature, 2003.

Pritchard, James B. *The Ancient Near East: Volume I, An Anthology of Texts and Pictures.* Princeton: Princeton University Press, 1958.

Rassmussen, Carl G. *Zondervan Atlas of the Bible.* Rev. ed. Grand Rapids: Zondervan, 2010.

Richter, Sandra L. *The Epic of Eden: A Christian Entry into the Old Testament.* Downers Grove, IL: IVP Academic, 2008.

Sahlins, Marshall. *Tribesmen: Foundations of Modern Anthropology.* Englewood Cliffs, NJ: Prentice Hall, 1968.

Sasson, Jack M. *Judges 1–12: A New Translation with Introduction and Commentary.* Anchor Yale Bible Commentaries. New Haven: Yale University Press, 2014.

Specter, Harvey. "Dog Fight." *Suits.* Season 1 episode 12.

Stager, Lawrence E. "The Song of Deborah—Why Some Tribes Answered the Call and Others Did Not." *Biblical Archaeology Review* 15.1 (1989): 51–55, 57–59, 62–64. https://library.biblicalarchaeology.org/article/the-song-of-deborah-why-some-tribes-answered-the-call-and-others-did-not/.

Stone, Lawson G. "Eglon's Belly and Ehud's Blade: A Reconsideration." *Journal of Biblical Literature* 128/4 (2009): 649–63.

———. *Judges.* Cornerstone Biblical Commentary. Vol. 3. Carol Stream, IL; Tyndale, 2012.

Wright, Christopher J. H. "The Ethical Authority of the Old Testament: A Survey of Approaches, Part 2." *Tyndale Bulletin* 43.2 (1992): 203–31. https://doi.org/10.53751/001c.30489.

Video Endnotes

Session 1 Video

Lawson G. Stone, *Judges*, Cornerstone Biblical Commentary, vol. 3 (Carol Stream, IL: Tyndale, 2012), 269.

See Stone, *Judges*, 269.

Gerhard von Rad, "The Beginnings of Historical Writing in Ancient Israel," in *The Problem of the Hexateuch and Other Essays* (London: SCM, 1966), 166–204.

Christopher J. H. Wright, "The Ethical Authority of the Old Testament: A Survey of Approaches, Part 2," *Tyndale Bulletin* 43.2 (1992), 228, https://doi.org/10.53751/001c .30489.

Session 3 Video

Lawson G. Stone, *Judges*, Cornerstone Biblical Commentary, vol. 3 (Carol Stream, IL: Tyndale, 2012), 269. (Emphasis added.)

Stone, *Judges*, 222. (Emphasis added.)

Stone, *Judges*, 222. (Emphasis added.)

Stone, *Judges*, 222. (Emphasis original.)

Becca Spradlin, "Avoiding Mission Drift: Four Ways to Cultivate Your Organization's Eternal Impact," CitygateNetwork.com, https://www.citygatenetwork.org/NewsBot .asp?MODE=VIEW&ID=2668.

Session 4 Video

Thomas R. Schreiner, "The Valuable Ministries of Women in the Context of Male Leadership: A Survey of Old and New Testament Examples and Teaching," in *Recovering Biblical Manhood and Womanhood: A Response to Evangelical Feminism* (Wheaton, IL: Crossway, 1991), 216.

Schreiner, "The Valuable Ministries of Women in the Context of Male Leadership," 217. (Emphasis added).

Schreiner, "The Valuable Ministries of Women in the Context of Male Leadership," 217. (Emphasis added.)

Schreiner, "The Valuable Ministries of Women in the Context of Male Leadership," 216.

Schreiner, "The Valuable Ministries of Women in the Context of Male Leadership," 216.

See Theodore Roosevelt's Speech at the Sorbonne Paris April 23, 1910, https://www.presidency.ucsb.edu/documents/address-the-sorbonne-paris-france-citizenship-republic; See Brené Brown's reflection on Roosevelt's speech "Brene Brown The Man in the Arena Speech" on YouTube. The quote here can be found at https://www.goodreads.com/quotes/10893896-there-are-a-million-cheap-seats-in-the-world-today.

Private conversation.

Session 5 Video

See James B. Pritchard, ed., *The Ancient Near East Vol. 1: An Anthology of Texts and Pictures* (Princeton: Princeton University Press, 1958), 175–182; esp. 180.

Anson F. Rainey and Steven Notley, *The Sacred Bridge: Carta's Atlas of the Biblical World* (Jerusalem: Carta, 2006), 137. See also Stone, *Judges*, 252.

S. Weingartner, "Chariots Changed Forever the Way Warfare Was Fought, Strategy Conceived and Empires Built," *Military Heritage* (August 1999), 19–27.

Personal communication.

Session 6 Video

Denis Baly, *The Geography of the Bible, new and revised ed.* (New York: Harper & Row, 1974), 146.

Session 7 Video

W. M. Thomson in Baly, *Geography of the Bible*, 146.

Gertrude Bell Archive, New Castle University, Letter from Gertrude Bell to her stepmother, Dame Florence Bell, February 1, 1905, https://gertrudebell.ncl.ac.uk/l/gb-1-1-1-1-15-5.

Session 8 Video

See Stone, *Judges*, 256.

Stone, *Judges*, 258.

Michelle Knight, "Geometry and Psalmody: Characterization and the Role of Deborah's Song

(Judges 5)" in "Now These Records are Ancient": Studies in Ancient Near Eastern and Biblical History, Language and Culture in Honor of K. Lawson Younger, Jr., ed. James K. Hoffmeier, Richard E. Averbeck, J. Caleb Howard and Wolfgang Zwickel, Ägypten und altes Testament 114 (Munster: Zaphon, 2022), 287–298, here 295.

Knight, "Geometry and Psalmody," 295.

United Nations Secretary-General António Guterres' 2019 report on "Conflict Related Sexual Violence."

Michele Lent Hirsch, "The Safest Prey: When Refugee Camps Become Sites of Violence," Women's Media Center, February 21, 2012, http://www.womensmediacenter.com /women-under-siege/the-safest-prey-when-refugee-camps-become-sites-of-violence.

Knight, "Geometry and Psalmody," 295.

Carolyn Moore, When Women Lead: Embrace Your Authority, Move Beyond Barriers, and Find Joy in Leading Others (Grand Rapids: Zondervan, 2022).

Stone, Judges, 269–70. (Emphasis added.)

Stone, Judges, 270. (Emphasis added.)

Stone, Judges, 270. (Emphasis added.)

Wright, "Ethical Authority of the Old Testament," 228, https://doi.org/10.53751/001c.30489.

About the Author

Dr. Sandra Richter is the Robert H. Gundry Chair of Biblical Studies at Westmont College. She earned her PhD from Harvard University in Hebrew Bible and her MA in Theological Studies from Gordon-Conwell Theological Seminary. She has taught at Asbury Theological Seminary, Wesley Biblical Seminary, and Wheaton College. Because of her passion for the real people and places of the biblical narrative, she has spent many years directing Israel Studies programs that focus on historical geography and field archaeology. Sandy has a heart for the church and bringing high scholarship to the body. She is best known for her book *The Epic of Eden: A Christian Entry into the Old Testament* and its associated Bible studies: Epic of Eden, Isaiah, Jonah, Ruth, and Psalms.

Also Available from Sandra Richter, PhD

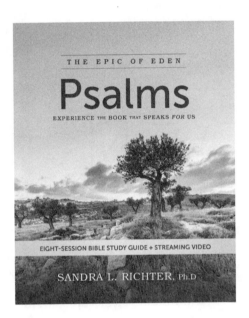

THE EPIC OF EDEN PSALMS

Experience fresh connections to contemporary worship and devotional practices.

You will discover:

- How to bridge the gap between the culture and practices of ancient Israel and today
- How you can come to God with all your emotions: grief, anger, praise, fear, and hope
- How and why the people of Israel used the Psalms in worship
- Why the book of Psalms is critical in our devotional lives today
- How the Psalms can empower your prayer life

Keep learning with the original Epic of Eden Video Study Series!

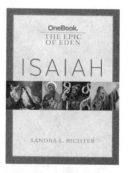

Sandra Richter's evocative and compelling *The Epic of Eden* series has helped thousands of churches and individual believers discover the deep beauty of the Old Testament, with the story of Jesus that lies in the heart of it. Legendary Bible stories take on new life as Dr. Richter clearly articulates their part of a larger pattern, revealing an even deeper significance for the stories individually.

Seedbed

Read what participants are saying:

"The entire *Epic of Eden* study series
has taken our church by storm."
–GREG F.

"I have class after class and small group
after small group asking to study
The Epic of Eden, along with *Ruth* and *Isaiah*."
–ROBIN P.

"This study is simply phenomenal.
Every single video session and the
weekly homework leave me covered in
goosebumps. Absolutely mind blowing!"
–JAN M.

"I don't think there has ever been or will ever be
a better series of lessons for my Sunday
school class than *The Epic of Eden*."
–JOY B.

You can find the original *Epic of Eden Video Study Guide*, along with
three focused installments on the books of *Isaiah*, *Jonah*, and *Ruth*,
all with excellent video sessions by Sandra Richter.

Available now at
epicofeden.com